Ramya Nagesh is a barrister at No5 Chambers, where she specialises in the full range of criminal matters. Ramya acts for both the Prosecution and the Defence, and represents both individuals and corporations. The vast majority of her criminal practice these days is in the Crown Court, but she also has experience in the Magistrates' Courts, and in the Court of Appeal.

Ramya sits as the independent legal representative on the West Midlands Hate Crime Scrutiny Panel. She is also a Trustee for Justice Is Now – a non-profit organisation seeking to make improvements to the ways in which sexual offences are treated in the criminal courts. Ramya is the author of the book: A Practical Guide to the Law in Relation to Hate Crime. She has also authored a number of articles on topics that include sleepwalking and the criminal law, international criminal law, hate crime and legal professional privilege.

Covid-19 and Criminal Law – The Essential Guide

Covid-19 and Criminal Law – The Essential Guide

Ramya Nagesh
Barrister (Lincoln's Inn),
LLB (Hons), MSc (LSE)

Law Brief Publishing

Published 2020 by Law Brief Publishing, an imprint of Law Brief Publishing Ltd
30 The Parks
Minehead
Somerset
TA24 8BT

www.lawbriefpublishing.com

Paperback: 978-1-913715-21-2

For all the victims of Covid-19

PREFACE

When 'lockdown' was announced on 23 March 2020, we might have been forgiven for assuming that it placed the brakes on the pace of modern life. Non-essential shops were closed, public houses and restaurants were empty and the streets were devoid of traffic, as people across the country were told to remain at home. However, the effect on the criminal law and the criminal justice system was quite the opposite. Almost overnight, new offences were brought into force. The criminal courts which – until that date – had operated almost entirely through in-person appearances, were hauled into a virtual forum. Jury trials were adjourned in their thousands, as those acting in them scrambled to conceive of a system that would allow them to continue.

It is important for all of us working within the criminal justice system to understand the changes that have been made, both in statute and in practice, and be aware of how this might impact upon the future of the criminal justice system.

This book serves as an essential guide to all those wishing to gain that insight. There is a great deal to consider; any section of this guide could quite easily become a book in its own right. However, as an essential guide, this book serves to provide an overview of the key issues.

It is split into three main parts. The first looks at criminal offences – the new offences created, and the impact of the pandemic on existing offences. The second looks at the court system itself – namely, virtual hearings, practical points for the practitioner and options to allow jury trials to resume. The third part considers the impact of Covid-19 on Judicial decisions, namely as to sentencing and bail decisions.

There have been differences in the ways in which all devolved powers have dealt with the pandemic. This book focuses on the law in England and Wales. Where there have been differences between the English and Welsh approaches, they are addressed separately.

As ever, the law is continually changing, and perhaps at no time in recent memory has it been changing as rapidly as now. I make it clear, therefore, that the law in this book is correct as of 30 June 2020.

Ramya Nagesh
June 2020

CONTENTS

PART ONE

CRIMINAL OFFENCES AND COVID-19

CHAPTER ONE
OVERVIEW OF THE CORONAVIRUS ACT AND REGULATIONS

This Chapter provides an overview of the Coronavirus Act 2020 and the corresponding English and Welsh Regulations, from a criminal law perspective. It sets out the key differences between them. It also considers what might constitute a 'reasonable excuse' under both the Act and the Regulations.

OVERVIEW

25 March 2020 marked just under two months since the first confirmed case of Covid-19 in the United Kingdom, two days since lockdown had officially taken hold of the country, and the day of commencement of the Coronavirus Act 2020 ("the Act"). It had flown through the Committees and the Houses to receive Royal Assent in only six days. Indeed, on the day that 'lockdown' was announced to the nation, the Act was only four days old, but had merely the House of Lords to face before it achieved Royal Assent. This passage was meteoric, compared to the usual trundling steps a Bill takes to achieve Act status.

Its sister Regulations in England – the Health Protection (Coronavirus, Restrictions) (England) Regulations 2020 ("the English Regulations") – came into force one day later, on 26 March 2020. Wales saw the publication of similar Regulations – the Health Protection (Coronavirus, Restrictions)(Wales) Regulations 2020 ("the Welsh Regulations") on the same day.

Whilst a rapidly implemented and robust legislative framework was arguably necessary for the situation in which the nation found itself, it did mean that lawyers and non-lawyers alike were grappling with a new set of laws, almost literally overnight. Of most importance to anyone working in the criminal justice system was the fact that those laws included a bundle of new criminal offences. A comprehensive grasp of those offences is something that all of us must acquire. Below, therefore, I set out the elements of the Act and the Regulations in England and Wales that are essential for anyone working with, or studying, the criminal law.

KEY DIFFERENCES BETWEEN THE ACT AND THE REGULATIONS

Both the Act and the Regulations contain criminal offences within them. Both are targeted at the current coronavirus pandemic. What, then, is the difference between the offences contained in them – and to what extent might there be overlap?

In the broadest terms, the Act creates offences committed by infectious or potentially infectious people who fail to comply with requirements designed to contain and treat the virus. The Regulations, by contrast, create offences committed by any person who fails to comply with the general standards set in place to ensure public safety (colloquially known as 'lockdown').

The Act sets out a framework to enable a) the effective containment and treatment of Covid-19; and b) the effective continuation of services and businesses. The criminal offences committed by individuals under the Act are those committed when a person, who is reasonably suspected to be infectious by certain officials, fails to comply with the powers exercised by those officials under that Act (for example, to direct the person to be assessed and screened). It follows that the offences under the Act can only be committed by a person who is reasonably suspected to be infectious. If there is no reasonable suspicion that a person is infectious, then the powers available to certain officials under the Act do not apply, and the person cannot be guilty of an offence for failing to comply with those powers. In other words, a constable cannot direct a person to attend an assessment centre, with no suspicion at all that the person is infectious – nor will that person commit an offence if they refuse to attend.

By contrast, the Regulations set out provisions to maintain general public safety, by (generally speaking) imposing restrictions on the movement of the public. These are rules to which all must abide, notwithstanding that there may be no reason to consider that the particular person is infectious. In that case, it is no defence to an offence under those Regulations to contend that the person was very clearly not infectious.

It is important to ensure that the defendant in a case brought under either the Act or the Regulations is charged under the correct instrument. A clear starting point is to determine whether the person was reasonably suspected of being infectious at the time. Where the person was not, then any prosecution brought under the Act cannot be supported.

WHAT CONSTITUTES A REASONABLE EXCUSE IN THE ACT AND THE REGULATIONS?

The concept of 'reasonable excuse' repeats itself throughout both the Act and the two sets of Regulations. What exactly constitutes a 'reasonable excuse'?

First, the burden of proof will fall upon the Prosecution to disprove reasonable excuse. In *R v John* [1974] 1 WLR 624, the Court - considering the offence of failing to provide a specimen without reasonable excuse - recognised that the burden of proof fell on the Prosecution: whilst it is for the defence to raise the excuse, it is for the Prosecution to negative it.

There is no exhaustive list of 'reasonable excuses' in the Act or the Regulations. However, some of the Regulations provide non-exhaustive examples that could be instructive when dealing with other Regulations or the Act. Regulation 6, for example, provides that a reasonable excuse for staying elsewhere than at your own home (or a linked home) might be: a) staying elsewhere to attend a funeral if you fall into one of the given categories of people; b) as an elite athlete, staying elsewhere for the purposes of training or competition; or c) staying elsewhere to provide care or assistance to a vulnerable person.

When considering what a 'reasonable excuse' may be in the context of other provisions, then, it may assist to draw upon those non-exhaustive lists to help give an idea of what might be considered 'reasonable'.

Secondly, we can turn to other uses of 'reasonable excuse' in the criminal law. The concept itself is not a new one. Those found in possession of an offensive weapon may absolve themselves if the Prosecution has not proven that their excuse for having it was not reasonable. Those defendants failing to provide a sample may only be convicted if they had no reasonable excuse for the failure.

In *Garry v CPS* (2019) EWHC 636 (Admin), it was said that whether the defence of reasonable excuse is made out depends on the facts of the case; the fact-finding tribunal enjoys a wide discretion.

Where the defendant has an honest but mistaken belief as to certain facts, which – if true – would amount to lawful authority to commit the act that he did, then that is capable of amounting to a reasonable excuse (*R v Terence Jones* (1995) 1 Cr App R 262).

What we can take from all of this, then, is that whether the defendant has a reasonable excuse for breaching the relevant provision will be a matter of judgment for the fact-finding tribunal, who enjoys wide discretion in the matter. In advancing an excuse as reasonable, it may assist to refer to other examples given within the Regulations – even where they do not directly apply to the Regulation the defendant is said to have breached. They provide some insight into the sort of exceptions that Parliament had in mind when it wrote in the 'reasonable excuse' provisions, though they cannot of themselves be decisive of whether the defendant had a reasonable excuse for breaching other provisions within the Act or the Regulations.

CHAPTER TWO
OFFENCES UNDER THE CORONAVIRUS ACT 2020

This chapter looks at the Coronavirus Act in detail, from a criminal law perspective. It sets out the new offences created under the Act in both England and Wales.

The Act is comprised of 545 pages, 102 Sections and 29 additional Schedules. Criminal justice workers and practitioners may be relieved to know that they can whittle their reading down to focus on Schedules 21 and 22. It is those Schedules that provide the criminal offences under the Act, with which those of us working in the criminal justice system will be dealing in practice. As this book is an essential guide to the criminal law, I shall focus on Schedules 21 and 22.

SCHEDULE 21 OF THE CORONAVIRUS ACT 2020

Schedule 21 confers powers relating to potentially infectious persons. Part 1 sets out definitions to be used through the rest of the Schedule. Paragraphs 6 to 22 of Part 2 set out the various powers now conferred upon certain individuals. Finally, Paragraph 23 of Part 2 crystallises the particular offences that can be committed under Schedule 21, along with the maximum sentence for all.

Part 1: Interpretation

Part 1 of Schedule 21 defines the terms that will permeate the rest of the Schedule. At paragraph 2, 'potentially infectious persons' are:

> "*2 Potentially infectious persons*
>
> *(1) For the purposes of this Schedule, a person is "potentially infectious" at any time if—*
>
> > *(a) the person is, or may be, infected or contaminated with coronavirus, and there is a risk that the person might infect or contaminate others with coronavirus, or*
> >
> > *(b) the person has been in an infected area within the 14 days preceding that time.*
>
> *(2) For the purposes of this paragraph, "infected area" means any country, territory or other area outside the United Kingdom which the Secretary of State has declared as a country, territory or area—*
>
> > *(a) where there is known or thought to be sustained human-to-human transmission of coronavirus, or*
> >
> > *(b) from which there is a high risk that coronavirus will be transmitted to the United Kingdom.*
>
> *(3) A declaration under sub-paragraph (2)—*
>
> > *(a) is to be made by being published online, and*
> >
> > *(b) must as soon as reasonably practicable after it is made, also be published in the London Gazette.*"

Paragraph 3 sets out other definitions relevant to Schedule 21:

"3 Other definitions

(1) In this Schedule—

"assessment", in relation to a person, means assessment of the measures that it would be appropriate to take in relation to the person (under this Schedule or otherwise) to mitigate the risk that the person might infect or contaminate others with coronavirus;

"biological sample" includes a sample of blood or respiratory secretions (including a sample of such secretions taken by a swab of the nasopharyngeal cavity);

"immigration officer" means a person appointed by the Secretary of State as an immigration officer under paragraph 1 of Schedule 2 to the Immigration Act 1971;

"screening", in relation to a person, means—

(a) assessing the extent to which a person has been exposed to coronavirus,

(b) determining whether the person is infected or contaminated with coronavirus, and

(c) assessing the person's symptoms and state of health.

(2) "Public health officer" means—

(a) in Part 2 of this Schedule—

(i) an officer of the Secretary of State designated by the Secretary of State for any or all of the purposes of this Schedule, or

(ii) a registered public health consultant so designated;

[…]

(c) in Part 4 of this Schedule—

(i) an officer of the Welsh Ministers designated by them for any or all of the purposes of this Schedule, or

(ii) a registered public health consultant so designated;

[…]

(3) A designation under sub-paragraph (2) may in particular be of a class or description of person.

(4) In this Schedule references to England, Scotland, Wales and Northern Ireland include the territorial sea adjacent to those parts of the United Kingdom respectively."

Part 2: Powers under Schedule 21

Part 2 of Schedule 21 sets out the powers available to certain officials.

The particular powers begin at paragraph 6. Paragraph 6 states that where a public health official has reasonable grounds to suspect that a person in England is potentially infectious, they may:

(a) Direct the person to go immediately to a specified place that is suitable for screening and assessment;

(b) Remove the person to a place suitable for screening and assessment; or

(c) Request a constable to remove the person to a place suitable for screening and assessment (and the constable may then do so).

These powers are, though, subject to the limitation that the officer may only exercise them if the officer considers it necessary and proportionate to do so:

(a) In the interests of the person;

(b) For the protection of other people; or

(c) For the maintenance of public health.

However, where the officer exercises these powers, the officer must tell the person who is to be subject to them: a) of the reason for directing or removing them; and b) that it is an offence to fail to comply or (where the person is removed) to abscond.

Paragraph 7 confers the same powers upon constables and immigration officers, subject to the same requirements that a) it be considered necessary and proportionate for any of the three given reasons; and b) the person is told the reason for the order and that it is an offence not to comply. However, paragraph 7 adds the additional requirement - at subparagraph 5 - that the immigration officer or constable must, before exercising the powers conferred by the paragraph, consult a public health officer "*to the extent that it is practicable to do so*".

Paragraph 8 then sets out the scope and limitations of paragraphs 9 to 11. Similarly to the preceding provisions, paragraphs 9 to 11 may be applied where a public health officer has reasonable grounds to suspect that the person is potentially infectious and considers that it is necessary and proportionate to exercise a power conferred by paragraphs 9 to 11: a) in the interests of the person; b) for the protection of other people; or c) for the maintenance of public health.

Paragraph 9 gives the public health officer the power to require a potentially infectious person to remain at the place for screening and assessment purposes for a period not exceeding 48 hours. As with previous provisions under Schedule 21, the officer must inform the person a) of the reason for imposing the requirement; b) of the maximum period the person may be required to remain there; and c) that it is an offence to fail to comply with the requirement. This imposition may be enforced by a public health officer or a constable keeping the person at the place.

Paragraph 10 gives the public health officer the power to require the potentially infectious person to be screened and assessed. It may also impose other requirements on that person in connection with their screening and assessment. This includes the requirement to provide a biological sample, and to answer questions about their health or other relevant matters, such as travel history.

Paragraph 11 allows the public health officer to direct the potentially infectious person to go to another specified place, remove the person to that place or request a constable to remove the person to that place, where the public health officer considers it "*appropriate*" for the purposes of screening or assessing the person.

Paragraph 12 then clarifies that where a person is moved to another place, paragraphs 9 to 11 apply in relation to that person afresh at that other place.

Paragraph 13 provides immigration officers and constables with the power to keep a potentially infectious person in a place until a public health officer can exercise their powers under paragraphs 9 to 11.

This therefore provides for a situation where a public health officer is not immediately available to assess the person and the situation. However, there are time limits. A constable may not keep a person for longer than 24 hours, unless an officer of superintendent rank or higher gives their consent to extend the period. In that case, the period may be extended for a further 24 hours. An immigration officer may not keep a person for longer than 3 hours, unless a chief immigration officer or higher gives their consent to extend the period. In that case, the period may be extended for a further 9 hours.

Again, where a person is kept in a place under this paragraph, they must be told of the reason for keeping them and that it is an offence to abscond. Furthermore, they must be told of the maximum period for which they may be kept, taking into account the potential extension periods. Finally, paragraph 13 provides that before exercising the powers to keep a person under this paragraph, the immigration officer or constable must consult a public health officer "*to the extent that it is practicable to do so*".

Paragraph 14 confers powers on a public health officer where a person has either been confirmed to have coronavirus, where their screening has been inconclusive or where a public health officer has assessed that person and has reasonable grounds to suspect that the person is potentially infectious. If any of these criteria are satisfied, then the public health officer may impose such "*requirements and restrictions*" on the person as the officer considers necessary and proportionate: a) in the interests of the person; b) for the protection of other people; or c) for the maintenance of public health. Paragraph 14 lists some requirements that may be included – for example, to provide contact details or to remain at a specified place in isolation from others for a specified period.

By way of paragraph 15, the period specified in relation to a requirement to remain or a restriction under paragraph 14 may not exceed 14 days. In any event, a public health officer must – if they have imposed a requirement to remain or restriction – assess the person within 48 hours and reconsider which requirements or restrictions it is necessary and proportionate to impose on that person. They may revoke or replace the requirement or restriction. Paragraph 16 then indicates that the requirement may be enforced by a constable or public health officer.

Paragraph 17 provides a right of appeal for the person on whom the requirement or restriction is imposed under paragraph 14.

Paragraph 18 sets out duties in relation to those responsible for children. In essence, they must – so far as reasonably practicable – secure that the child complies with any direction, instruction, requirement or restriction given to or imposed on the child under Part 2 of Schedule 21.

Paragraph 19 deals with formalities (i.e. that the instruction may be given orally or in writing - but if given orally, must be followed by written notice). Paragraph 20 deals with ancillary powers of a public health officer, constable or immigration officer. They may, under that paragraph, give reasonable instructions to a person in connection with a direction given to a potentially infectious person, or the removal of that person. Paragraph 21 states that a person exercising a power under Part 2 must have regard to any relevant guidance issued, and any advice given by a public health officer in relation to any particular case.

Finally, paragraph 22 confirms that when the 'transmission control period' comes to an end, any requirement or restriction imposed under the power ceases to have effect.

Part 2 Paragraph 23: Offences

Paragraph 23 of Part 2 sets out the offences that can be committed by a person in relation to Part 2. In essence, should a public health officer, immigration officer or constable exercise their powers legitimately under the preceding provisions, it is an offence to fail to comply, to abscond (or attempt to abscond), or to knowingly provide false or misleading information. The paragraph states as follows:

> "*(1) A person commits an offence if the person—*
>
> > *(a) fails without reasonable excuse to comply with any direction, reasonable instruction, requirement or restriction given to or imposed on the person under this Part of this Schedule,*
> >
> > *(b) fails without reasonable excuse to comply with a duty under paragraph 18(1) or (2) (duties of individuals who have responsibility for a child),*
> >
> > *(c) absconds or attempts to abscond while being removed to or kept at a place under this Part of this Schedule,*
> >
> > *(d) knowingly provides false or misleading information in response to a requirement to provide information under this Part of this Schedule or otherwise in connection with the exercise of any power under this Part of this Schedule, or*
> >
> > *(e) obstructs a person who is exercising or attempting to exercise a power conferred by this Part of this Schedule.*
>
> *(2) A person guilty of an offence under this paragraph is liable on summary conviction to a fine not exceeding level 3 on the standard scale.*"

PART 4 OF SCHEDULE 21: WALES

Part 4 of Schedule 21 provides like provisions (as Part 2) in relation to Wales.

Paragraph 48 allows the Welsh Ministers the power to make a declaration as to the threat risk of coronavirus at any point, in a similar way as the power conferred upon the Secretary of State under Part 2.

Paragraphs 50 to 67 mirror paragraphs 6 to 23, but apply to Wales, rather than England. The powers conferred upon constables, public health officials and immigration officials are the same. The people against whom such powers might be exercised are those who are reasonably suspected of being potentially infectious. It follows that the elements of the offences that the prosecution must prove are the same as those under the provisions applying to England.

WHAT DO THE PROSECUTION NEED TO PROVE IN PROSECUTING A SCHEDULE 21 OFFENCE?

The Prosecution needs to prove the following, when prosecuting an offence under Parts 2 (England) or 4 (Wales) of Schedule 21 to the Act:

- That the defendant was made subject to a requirement, direction etc., under the relevant section of the Act;
- The person making the requirement was an immigration officer, constable or public health official (note that different sections apply to different officers);

- That the person making the requirement reasonably believed the defendant to be potentially infectious;
- That the requirement was valid, and did not contravene any restrictions placed upon the scope of the requirement[1];
- That the defendant either failed to comply with a requirement, *and* had no reasonable excuse for doing so; *or*
- Absconded, or attempted to abscond; *or*
- provided false or misleading information in response to a requirement to provide information, *and* did so knowingly; *or*
- Obstructed a person exercising or attempting to exercise a power under Schedule 21.

It is important to note that the person making the requirement must have reasonably believed the defendant to be potentially infectious. If that belief was not, or could not have been, present then the prosecution has a fatal gap, and should fail. This is important; it ensures that the power to impose potentially onerous restrictions and requirements on individuals is limited, so far as possible, to those who might reasonably be thought to actually be at risk to others and to themselves by carrying the virus.

Furthermore, note that the prosecution must prove that the defendant had no reasonable excuse for failure to comply with a

1 For example, paragraphs 15 (England) and 59 (Wales) specify that the direction to remain in a place cannot require the person to remain for longer than 14 days. If the direction does in fact require the person to remain in place for longer than 14 days, it is likely to be argued successfully that either the Prosecution have failed to prove that a valid requirement was imposed or, alternatively, that the Defendant had a reasonable excuse for failing to comply

restriction. The concept of 'reasonable excuse' is repeated in Schedule 22 and then, once more, in the Regulations. I analyse it further under a separate heading in this chapter; for that reason I shall not delve further into the concept at this point.

SCHEDULE 22 OF THE CORONAVIRUS ACT 2020

Schedule 22 confers powers in relation to events, gatherings and premises. Paragraph 9 of that Schedule creates an offence of failing to comply, without a reasonable excuse, with a prohibition, requirement or restriction imposed by a direction under Schedule 22.

Part 1: Interpretation

Similarly to the approach in Schedule 21, Part 1 of Schedule 22 deals with interpretation of the rest of the Schedule and general matters. Part 2 of the Schedule sets out the substantive powers in relation to events, gatherings and premises.

Of most relevance in Part 1 of Schedule 22 is the fact that 'premises' is defined as:

> " *"premises" includes any place and, in particular, includes –*
>
> *(a) Any vehicle, train, vessel or aircraft,*
>
> *(b) Any tent or movable structure, and*
>
> *(c) Any offshore installation (within the meaning given by regulation 3 of the Offshore Installations and Pipeline Works*

(Management and Administration) Regulations 1995 (S.I. 1995/738),

And references to premises include a part of premises;"

Paragraph 2 of Part 1 makes clear that nothing in Schedule 22 applies in relation to the Parliamentary Estate.

Part 2: Powers Relating to Events, Gatherings and Premises in England

Part 2 of Schedule 22 provides powers to the Secretary of State to make rules in relation to events, gatherings and premises in England.

To start with, paragraph 3 essentially provides that the Secretary of State may at any time make a declaration to the effect that coronavirus constitutes a serious and imminent threat to public health in England, and that the powers in Schedule 22 will be an effective means of either controlling the incidence or transmission of coronavirus in England or facilitating the most appropriate deployment of medical or emergency personnel and resources.

Paragraph 4 clarifies that references to 'public health response period' in Schedule 22 are references to a period which begins when the Secretary of State makes a declaration under paragraph 3, and ends when the Secretary of State revokes that declaration.

We then move to the particular powers. Paragraph 5 relates to powers to restrict the holding of an event or gathering in England.

Paragraphs 5(1) and 5(2) provide:

"*(1) The Secretary of State may, for the purpose of—*

> *(a) preventing, protecting against, delaying or otherwise controlling the incidence or transmission of coronavirus, or*
>
> *(b) facilitating the most appropriate deployment of medical or emergency personnel and resources,*
>
> *issue a direction prohibiting, or imposing requirements or restrictions in relation to, the holding of an event or gathering in England.*
>
> *(2) A direction under sub-paragraph (1) may be issued in relation to—*
>
> *(a) a specified event or gathering, or*
>
> *(b) events or gatherings of a specified description."*

This power is limited by paragraph 5(3) of Schedule 22 – under paragraph 5(3), the direction can only impose prohibitions, requirements or restrictions on:

(a) The owner or occupier of premises for an event or gathering to which the direction relates;

(b) The organiser of such an event or gathering;

(c) Any other person involved in holding such an event or gathering.

So it is that only those who are, in some way, responsible for the event or gathering who may have prohibitions imposed on them in relation to that gathering; it follows that only they may be held responsible should the gathering continue in contravention of the direction. Paragraph 5(7) clarifies that a person whose only involvement is attending the event or gathering is not to fall under the otherwise apparently wide provision of 'any other person involved in holding such an event or gathering' under paragraph 5(3)(c).

Paragraphs 5(4), 5(5) and 5(6) provide clarification as to the application of the power. Paragraph 5(4) of Schedule 22 states that the direction may only be issued during a 'public health response period' (which we have seen defined in Part 1). Paragraph 5(5) of Schedule 22 states that the direction may include requirements about informing persons planning to attend about its prohibition or other restrictions. Therefore, a person organising a party might be required to inform all the invitees of the restrictions placed upon it, or the fact that it is a prohibited party. Finally, paragraph 5(6) of Schedule 22 clarifies that events or gatherings may be described by reference to a number of people attending the event or gathering, by reference to a requirement for medical or emergency services to attend, or "*in any other way*".

Paragraph 6 provides the Secretary of State with powers to close premises in England, or to impose restrictions on persons entering or remaining in them. Paragraphs 6(1) and 6(2) provide:

> "*(1) The Secretary of State may, for the purpose of—*
>
> *(a) preventing, protecting against, delaying or otherwise controlling the incidence or transmission of coronavirus, or*
>
> *(b) facilitating the most appropriate deployment of medical or emergency personnel and resources,*
>
> *issue a direction imposing prohibitions, requirements or restrictions in relation to the entry into, departure from, or location of persons in, premises in England.*

(2) A direction under sub-paragraph (1) may be issued in relation to—

(a) specified premises, or

(b) premises of a specified description."

As with paragraph 5 above, paragraph 6(3) limits the powers of the Secretary of State in terms of on whom the prohibitions, requirements or restrictions may be imposed:

(a) The owner or occupier of premises to which the direction relates;

(b) Any other person involved in managing entry into, or departure from, such premises or the location of persons in them.

Once again, the direction may only be issued during a public health response period (paragraph 6(4) of Schedule 22).

Paragraph 6(5) provides a non-exhaustive list of requirements. "*Among other things*", the direction may impose requirements for the purpose of: a) closing the premises; b) restricting entry into the premises; or c) securing restrictions in relation to the location of persons in the premises.

Paragraph 7 of Schedule 22 simply provides that the Secretary of State may vary or revoke, to any extent, a direction issued under Part 2 of Schedule 22.

Paragraph 8 deals with procedural matters in issuing a direction. The practitioner should be aware of this paragraph, though, as it sets out a number of mandatory requirements for the imposition of a direction. It may be, then, that if those arguments have not been complied with, argument could be made that it was not valid, and so no offence can have been committed. In summary, under paragraph 8:

i. The Secretary of State must have regard to any relevant advice from the Chief Medical Officer or any of the Deputy Chief Medical Officers of the Department of Health and Social Care, before issuing a direction under Part 2 of Schedule 22;

ii. Where a direction imposes prohibitions, requirements or restrictions on a person specific by name, the direction must be given in writing to that person and may be published in a manner the Secretary of State considers appropriate to bring it to the attention of others who may be affected;

iii. In any other case (i.e. the direction does not specify the subject of it by name), the direction must be published in a manner that the Secretary of State considers appropriate to bring it to the attention of those who may be affected by it;

iv. If the Secretary of State varies or revokes a direction to a person specified by name, then that person must be given notice in writing, and may be published in any other such manner to bring it to the attention of people who may be affected by it;

v. If the Secretary of State varies or revokes a direction in any other instance (i.e. not specifying the subject of it by name) then notice of the variation or revocation must be published in a way that is appropriate to bring it to the attention of persons who may be affected.

Paragraphs 9 and 10 of Schedule 22: Offences

Paragraphs 9 and 10 then create the offences that arise out of a failure to comply with directions issued by the Secretary of State under Schedule 22.

Paragraph 9 provides:

> "*(1) A person commits an offence if the person fails without reasonable excuse to comply with a prohibition, requirement or restriction imposed on the person by a direction issued under this Part of this Schedule.*
>
> *(2) A person guilty of an offence under this paragraph is liable on summary conviction to a fine.*"

Paragraph 10 addresses the situation where an offence under paragraph 9 is committed by a body corporate. Essentially, where the offence is proven to have been committed with the consent or connivance of an officer of the corporate body, or is proven to be attributable to any neglect on the part of such an officer, then the officer and the body corporate are guilty of the offence. By paragraph 10(2), 'officer' means a director, manager, secretary or other similar officer of the body corporate.

PART 4: WALES

Part 4 of Schedule 22 creates like provisions as Part 2, but applicable to Wales.

Paragraphs 28 to 33 mirror paragraphs 5 to 10 of Part 2 but apply to those within Wales. Therefore, the requirements placed upon the form of communicating a direction, and the restrictions as to who may be the subject of the direction, are exactly the same as those in England. Both in England and in Wales, a person may not be found guilty of failure to comply if they have a reason for so not doing.

WHAT DO THE PROSECUTION NEED TO PROVE IN PROSECUTING A SCHEDULE 22 OFFENCE?

In bringing a case under Part 2 or Part 4 of Schedule 22 of the Act, the Prosecution will need to prove the following:

- A direction was issued by the Secretary of State;
- The direction was issued during a public health response period (as defined in Part 1);
- The procedural requirements in paragraph 8 (England) or paragraph 31 (Wales) were complied with (e.g. notice of the direction was given in writing, if to a named person);
- The defendant falls into one of the categories of people who can be subject to a direction under paragraphs 5 and 6 (England) or 28 and 29 (Wales). In relation to paragraph 5 (England) or 28 (Wales), this is broadly a person involved with the organisation or running of a gathering. In relation to paragraph 6 (England) or 29 (Wales), this is a person who owns, occupies or manages entry into / departure from a premises;
- The defendant failed to comply with the direction;
- The defendant did not have a reasonable excuse for failing to comply.

By and large, those elements will be relatively straightforward to prove, or to accept the absence of. For example, it should not be too difficult for the Prosecution to provide evidence that notice of a direction was given in writing. If it were not, the absence of such a notice may well mean that the prosecution fails at an early stage. In fact, it may be that the only element which might be the cause of a contest in Court is the 'reasonable excuse' provision.

The 'reasonable excuse' provision is included as part of the statement of the offence, and thus one of the factors that the prosecution must prove. The question of what might constitute a 'reasonable excuse' to hold a gathering, or keep a premises open in contravention of a direction, is an interesting one. Unlike in the Regulations (as we shall see), no example is given of what might constitute a 'reasonable excuse'.

The concept of 'reasonable excuse' rears its head in both the Act and the Regulations, yet is accompanied by relatively little guidance within those documents as to what might constitute a 'reasonable excuse'. For that reason, I consider what might constitute a 'reasonable excuse' in Chapter One, and so will not delve into it again here.

CHAPTER THREE
OFFENCES UNDER THE CORONAVIRUS REGULATIONS 2020

This chapter looks at the English and Welsh Coronavirus Regulations 2020, from a criminal law perspective. It sets out the various obligations in the Regulations, that could lead to criminal proceedings if breached, as well as those regulations that actually create the offences.

The English Regulations came into force on 26 March 2020. The Welsh Regulations came into force on the same day.

CRIMINAL OFFENCES UNDER THE ENGLISH REGULATIONS

Regulation 9 makes it a criminal offence to contravene regulations 4 to 8, as well as to obstruct someone carrying out their duty under the Regulations.

An important note: although Regulation 9 has remained the same since it began, the Regulations which it makes it an offence to breach have undergone some changes. In this climate, more than any other in recent history, a few weeks can mean the difference between one set of obligations and another. Where a person is accused of committing an offence under these Regulations, therefore, it will be all the more important for the police, practitioners, and Judges to check which form of the Regulations was in force. Practitioners should also be sure that the behaviour complained of was actually prohibited at the time.

Regulation 3: 'emergency period'

Regulation 3 specifies that the term 'emergency period', which repeats itself throughout the remainder of the document, is the period beginning on the date that the Regulations come into force, and ending on a date specified by the Secretary of State.

Regulation 4: Restrictions on Certain Business Premises

Regulation 4 relates to the requirement to close premises and businesses during the emergency. It confers duties on those people who are responsible for carrying on a business (as specified in Part 1 of Schedule 2 of the Regulations). It states that, during the emergency period, a person responsible for carrying on such a business must a) close any premises, or part of the premises, in which food or drink are sold for consumption on the premises; and b) cease selling food or drink for consumption on its premises; or c) if it sells food or drink for consumption off the premises, cease selling food or drink for consumption on its premises. Under Regulation 4(2), room service does not count as 'being sold for consumption on the premises'. Regulation 4(3) clarifies that an area adjacent to the premises of the business where seating is made available for customers (whether or not by the business), is treated as part of the premises of that business.

In reality, that means that public houses, restaurants, cafes and other such premises had to stop their on-site services. This did not prevent them selling food or drink for take-away, and some continued to do so. Additionally, this does not prevent shops that sell food or drink for consumption off the premises continuing to do so.

Regulation 4(4) applies to other types of commercial business including nightclubs, cinemas, spas, hair salons and gyms. Under Regulation 4(4), the person responsible for carrying on such a business or providing such a service must cease to carry on that business or to provide that service during the emergency period. This effectively prevented, for example, a hairdresser continuing to provide hairdressing services despite closing their premises.

Exceptions are provided for in Regulation 4(5). In summary, it exempts a) premises used to broadcast a performance over the Internet, radio or television; b) suitable premises used to host blood donation sessions; c) facilities for training elite athletes.

Regulation 5: Restrictions on Other Business Premises

Regulation 5 applies to businesses providing library services, and businesses providing holiday accommodation. Until 15 June 2020, it applied to a wider range of businesses; it has since been amended.

Regulation 5(1) provides that a person responsible for providing library services must cease to do so except by making deliveries in response to orders made online, by telephone or by post. The premises must be closed, and people should not be admitted who is not required to provide delivery services.

Under Regulation 5(2), though, libraries may operate a book shop, and a café that either provides off-site premises or is itself separate from the library premises.

Regulations 5(3) and 5(4) provide that a person responsible for premises that provide holiday accommodation must cease to provide those services, apart from the following:

> "*(4) A person referred to in paragraph (3) may continue to carry on their business and keep any premises used in that business open —*
>
> *(a) to provide accommodation for any person, who—*
>
> *(i) is unable to return to their main residence;*
>
> *(ii) uses that accommodation as their main residence;*
>
> *(iii) needs accommodation while moving house;*
>
> *(iv) needs accommodation to attend a funeral;*
>
> *(v) is isolating themselves from others as required by law;*
>
> *(vi) is an elite athlete, the coach of an elite athlete, or (in the case of an elite athlete who is under the age of 18), the parent of an elite athlete, and needs accommodation for the purposes of training or competition;*
>
> *(aa) to provide accommodation for any person—*
>
> *(i) who works in one of the critical sectors listed in the guidance titled "Guidance for critical workers who can access schools or educational settings" published by the Cabinet Office and the Department for Education and updated on 5th May 20208, and*
>
> *(ii) whose need for accommodation is connected to their work;*

(b) to provide accommodation or support services for the homeless,

(c) to host blood donation sessions, or

(d) for any purpose requested by the Secretary of State, or a local authority."

Regulation 6: Restrictions on Movement

Regulation 6 places restrictions on staying overnight at another house. Following developments in mid-June 2020, people who live alone are no longer restricted to staying in their own household. Certain people who live alone have been able to link with another household. Therefore, they are able to stay overnight at either their own house or their linked household. This prohibition is subject to the caveat that the person may stay elsewhere if they have a reasonable excuse for so doing.

Regulation 6(2) provides some examples of what might constitute a 'reasonable excuse' under this provision:

i. Attending the funeral of a member of their household, close family or (if nobody from those categories is attending) a friend of the deceased;

ii. Where the person is an elite athlete, and they need to stay elsewhere for training or competition purposes;

iii. The person is moving house;

iv. The person needs to stay elsewhere for work purposes or certain specified caring purposes;

v. The person needs to stay elsewhere to attend a birth;

vi. The person needs to stay elsewhere to fulfil a legal obligation;

vii. The person is a child and needs to stay with their parents at separate residences;

viii. The person is unable to return to their home (for example, for safety reasons).

The prohibition on staying outside the household does not apply to a person who is homeless. This avoids the problem of attempting to artificially assign a legal 'household' to someone who is ordinarily of no fixed abode. Not only would this not represent the reality, but without an actual household to which the homeless person can affix themselves, they would inevitably be criminalised repeatedly for sleeping on the streets or in temporary accommodation. This cannot be in the interests of either the person or the effective administration of justice.

Regulation 7: Gatherings and 7A: Linked Households

Regulation 7 restricts gatherings. Under Regulation 7(1), no person may participate in a gathering outdoors of six or more people, or a gathering indoors of two or more people. This is, by virtue of Regulation 7(2), subject to certain exceptions. The first exception is that all the persons in the gathering are members of the same household. The second relates to people attending funerals, as members of the deceased's household, or close family or friends. The third is an exception to allow elite athletes to gather with their coaches or parents, when necessary for training or competition. The final exception is where the gathering is 'reasonably necessary' for a number of reasons that include work purposes, the provision of voluntary or charitable services, facilitating a house move, providing care or assistance to a vulnerable person, to enable one or more persons in the gathering to avoid injury or illness or escape risk of harm, or to fulfil a legal obligation or participate in legal proceedings.

Regulation 7(3) defines both 'gathering' and 'indoors'. A 'gathering' is when two or more people are present in the same place to engage in any form of social interaction or activity with each other. Thus, being in a park where numerous others are present is not a gathering. Meeting a group of friends in the park to have a picnic or a walk is a gathering. This avoids the clumsy situation where an unconnected group of strangers fall foul of the gathering restrictions simply because they happen to have gone to the same open area.

'Indoors' means a place that is enclosed, or substantially enclosed, as in Section 2 of the Health Act 2006, under the Smoke Free (Premises and Enforcement) Regulations 2006. In other words, those premises that are considered 'indoors' for the purposes of the smoking ban are considered to be 'indoors' for the purposes of the gatherings restriction.

Regulation 7A provides that a person living alone may 'link' to another household. The number of people living in the second household is not subject to any limit.

Regulation 8: Enforcement

Regulation 8 deals with enforcement of the preceding provisions. It provides that a 'relevant person' may take such action as is necessary to enforce Regulations 4 to 7.

Regulation 8(12) defines a 'relevant person' as follows:

> "*(12) For the purposes of this regulation—*
>
> *(a) a "relevant person" means—*
>
> *(i) a constable,*
>
> *(ii) a police community support officer,*
>
> *(iii) subject to paragraph (13), a person designated by a local authority for the purposes of this regulation, or*
>
> *(iv) a person designated by the Secretary of State for the purposes of this regulation;*
>
> *(b) references to a requirement include references to a restriction.*"

Regulation 8 sets out particular powers that a 'relevant person' may exercise in relation to the different preceding provisions.

In relation to breaches of Regulations 4 and 5, the relevant person may give the person a prohibition notice if the 'relevant person' reasonably believes the person is contravening Regulation 4 or 5, and a prohibition notice is necessary to prevent continued contravention (see Regulation 8(2)).

In relation to breaches of Regulation 6(1), the relevant person may direct that person to return to where they are living (see Regulation 8(3)). If the person staying in a place they should not be is a child, then it is the individual with responsibility for that child, and who is accompanying the child at the time of the breach, who may be directed to take the child back to their home (Regulations 8(4) to 8(7)). These actions taken in relation to breaches of Regulation 6(1), though, must only be done so if the relevant person considers that it is a necessary and proportionate means of ensuring compliance.

In relation to breaches of Regulation 7, the relevant person may: a) direct the gathering to disperse; b) direct any person in the gathering to return to the place where they are living; c) remove any person in the gathering to the place where they are living (see Regulation 8(9)). If the relevant person is removing a person in the gathering, the Regulations explicitly state that they may use reasonable force (see Regulation 8(10)). Where the person in breach is a child, it is the individual with responsibility for them who may be directed to take the child to their home (see Regulations 8(10A) and (10B)).

As with breaches of Regulation 6(1), the relevant person must only exercise their powers where it is necessary and proportionate to ensure compliance (Regulation 8(10C)). This would mean that a relevant person should not remove someone forcibly from a gathering where that person would comply with a direction to leave. It could not, after all, ever be necessary and proportionate to use force to ensure compliance where words complete the task. It has the effect, then, of establishing an order of the actions that may be taken on the part of the relevant person. First, they should ask the gathering to disperse, which may be all that is necessary to ensure compliance. If that is ignored and so does not ensure compliance, it may then be necessary and proportionate to direct one or more people to return home. Only where neither of those measures ensure compliance might it then become necessary and proportionate to physically remove one or more persons from the gathering.

Regulation 9: Offences and Penalties

Regulations 4 to 7 establish restrictions imposed upon all members of the public. Regulation 8 establishes the rights of certain persons to impose those restrictions without recourse to the criminal courts. Regulation 9 establishes the offences that can be committed when breaching any of those earlier Regulations.

Regulation 9 states, in full:

> "***9.— Offences and penalties***
>
> *(1) A person who—*
>
> > *(a) without reasonable excuse contravenes a requirement in regulation 4, 5, 7 or 8, or*
> >
> > *(b) contravenes a requirement in regulation 6,*
>
> *commits an offence.*
>
> *(2) A person who obstructs, without reasonable excuse, any person carrying out a function under these Regulations, including any person who is a relevant person for the purposes of regulation 8, commits an offence.*
>
> *(3) A person who, without reasonable excuse, contravenes a direction given under regulation 8, or fails to comply with a reasonable instruction or a prohibition notice given by a relevant person under regulation 8, commits an offence.*
>
> *(4) An offence under this regulation is punishable on summary conviction by a fine.*
>
> *(5) If an offence under this regulation committed by a body corporate is proved—*

(a) to have been committed with the consent or connivance of an officer of the body, or

(b) to be attributable to any neglect on the part of such an officer,

the officer (as well as the body corporate) is guilty of the offence and liable to be prosecuted and proceeded against and punished accordingly.

(6) In paragraph (5), "officer" , in relation to a body corporate, means a director, manager, secretary or other similar officer of the body corporate.

(7) Section 24 of the Police and Criminal Evidence Act 19842 applies in relation to an offence under this regulation as if the reasons in subsection (5) of that section included—

(a) to maintain public health;

(b) to maintain public order.

(8) For the purposes of this regulation, references to a requirement include references to a restriction."

First, it is an offence to contravene a requirement under Regulations 4, 5, 7 or 8 without a reasonable excuse. By virtue of Regulation 9(8), 'requirement' includes 'restriction'. Therefore, a person should not:

(a) Open a business that they are prohibited from opening;

(b) Use a business premises for prohibited purposes (e.g. offering on-site consumption rather than simply take-away);

(c) Participate in a gathering larger than that allowed; or

(d) Fail to comply with a requirement imposed by a relevant person under section 8;

Unless they have a reasonable excuse.

No example is given in section 9 as to what a reasonable excuse for contravening these provisions might be. It should be noted that the earlier provisions have certain inbuilt exceptions already (e.g. Regulation 7 provides that a person may attend a gathering where they are attending a funeral in a certain capacity, or the person is providing care and assistance). Where that exception applies, the person cannot contravene Regulation 7(1). It follows that 'reasonable excuse' must be something separate and distinct from the inbuilt statutory exceptions.

Secondly, it is an offence to contravene a requirement in regulation 6 (staying overnight in a household that is not your own, or a 'linked' household). In the case of that offence, there is no 'reasonable excuse' provision in section 9; this is likely because Regulation 6 itself provides that a person is not prevented from staying outside their home where they have a reasonable excuse.

Thirdly, it is an offence to obstruct a person carrying out their duties under these Regulations, including a 'relevant person'. An example of that might be obstructing a police officer who is trying to disperse a gathering.

Finally, a person who fails to comply, without reasonable excuse, with a direction or prohibition notice under Regulation 8 commits an offence. Once more, then, we see that there is provision made to excuse those who may have a reasonable excuse for contravening the requirements.

There are two points worthy of note in the remaining provisions of Regulation 9. First, Regulation 9(7) extends section 24 of the Police and Criminal Evidence Act 1984 ("the 1984 Act") to apply to offences under Regulation 9. Section 24 of the 1984 Act relates to a constable's powers of arrest without a warrant; that power is therefore extended to allow the constable increased powers of arrest under the Regulations.

Secondly, the offences under Regulation 9 are triable only summarily. The punishment that can be meted out upon conviction is a fine only. However, Magistrates' Courts do now have the power to impose unlimited fines, as a result of section 85 of the Legal Aid, Sentencing and Punishment of Offenders Act 2012. Of course, the financial means of the defendant will form part of the assessment of the fine. However, where the defendant is of significant means, and their breaches warrant a serious sentence, they might feasibly face a hefty fine. This might be the case where, for example, a company is found to have repeatedly served food and drink on its premises in contravention of the restrictions in Rule 4.

Regulation 10: Fixed Penalty Notices

Regulation 10 deals with fixed penalty notices. Regulation 10(1) and (2) states:

> "***10.— Fixed penalty notices***
>
> *(1) An authorised person may issue a fixed penalty notice to anyone that the authorised person reasonably believes—*
>
> > *(a) has committed an offence under these Regulations;*
> >
> > *(b) is aged 18 or over.*

> *(2) A fixed penalty notice is a notice offering the person to whom it is issued the opportunity of discharging any liability to conviction for the offence by payment of a fixed penalty to an authority specified in the notice.*"

Regulation 10(11) defines 'authorised person' as follows:

> "*(11) In this regulation—*
>
> *(a) "authorised person" means—*
>
> *(i) a constable;*
>
> *(ii) a police community support officer;*
>
> *(iii) a person designated by the Secretary of State for the purposes of this regulation;*
>
> *(iv) subject to paragraph (12), a person designated by the relevant local authority for the purposes of this regulation;*"

The amount of the fixed penalty notice is £100 to be paid in 28 days, which is reduced to £50 if paid in 14 days (see Regulation 10(6) and (7)(a)). If the person has received a fixed penalty notice before for offences under the Regulations, however, the amount is doubled for each subsequent fixed penalty notice. This is capped at £3200 for the sixth, and subsequent, fixed penalty notices (see Regulation 10(7)(b)).

CRIMINAL OFFENCES UNDER THE WELSH REGULATIONS

On the whole, the Welsh Regulations mirror the English ones. However, there are some key differences; the main ones are that the requirement to maintain a two metre distance is enshrined in the Welsh Regulations, whereas the English Regulations stay silent as to that.

The criminal offences in the Welsh Regulations are set out in Regulation 12. There are offences created in relation to Regulations 4, 5, 6, 6A, 7, 8, 8A, 8B and 9. As above, I have not set out every Regulation that appears in the document – but focused on those which will be of use to those of us working in the criminal justice system.

As with the English Regulations, I emphasise an important point: although Regulation 12 has remained the same since it began, the Regulations which it makes it an offence to breach have undergone some changes. In this climate, more than any other in recent history, a few weeks can mean the difference between one set of obligations and another. Where a person is accused of committing an offence under these Regulations, therefore, it will be all the more important for the police, practitioners, and Judges to check which form of the Regulations was in force at the time of the alleged offence, and be sure that the behaviour complained of was actually prohibited at the time.

Regulation 4: Restrictions on Businesses

Regulation 4 of the Welsh Regulations differs from the English Regulations in the way it approaches certain businesses listed in Schedule 1. These include nightclubs, concert halls, casinos and hair salons.

Rather than prohibiting their operation, it allows their operation but mandates the following at section 5B:

> "*(5B) Where this paragraph applies, the person responsible for carrying on the business or providing the service must, during the emergency period, take all reasonable measures to ensure —*
>
> > *(a) that a distance of 2 metres is maintained between any persons on the premises (except between two members of the same household, or a carer and the person assisted by the carer),*
> >
> > *(b) that persons are only admitted to the premises in sufficiently small numbers to make it possible to maintain that distance, and*
> >
> > *(c) that a distance of 2 metres is maintained between persons waiting to enter the premises (except between two members of the same household, or a carer and the person assisted by the carer).*"

Regulation 5: Restrictions on Other Businesses

Regulation 5 of the Welsh Regulations does not apply to libraries, unlike its English counterpart. It focuses on holiday and camping premises. In essence, those businesses providing hotel, camping, or other such holiday accommodation must not continue to operate the business. The exceptions are: (i) to provide accommodation to those unable to return to their main residence or who use it as their main residence; (ii) to carry on the business by providing information or other services online, by telephone or by post (see Regulation 5(3) and (3A)). However, the person must take reasonable measures to ensure that a two metre distance maintained between those not of the same household, and they do not admit too many people to be able to respect that rule.

Regulation 6: Restrictions on Shops

Regulation 6 of the Welsh Regulations applies to shops and certain other businesses (including off licences and food shops). Regulation 6 of the Welsh Regulations states that the person responsible for carrying on the business, or providing the service, must take all reasonable measures to ensure the maintenance of a two metre distance. This includes only allowing in people in sufficiently small numbers to be able to maintain the distance.

Regulation 6A: Restriction on Places of Work

This Regulation provides that a person responsible for a place where people are working must, when such work is being carried out during the emergency period, take all reasonable measures to ensure that a two metre distance is maintained by people on the premises (unless they are part of the same household or are a carer and charge).

Regulation 7: Restrictions on Places of Worship, Crematoriums and Community Centres

Under Regulation 7, a place of worship must be closed, except for certain specified activities, provided that reasonable measures are taken to ensure that a two metre distance is maintained. These activities include the solemnization of a marriage or civil partnership, funerals or individual prayer (i.e. not communal prayer services).

Regulation 8: Restrictions on Movement and Being Indoors

Regulation 8(1) states:

> "*(1) During the emergency period, no person may, without reasonable excuse—*
>
> *(a) leave the area local to the place where they are living or remain away from that area;*
>
> *(b) gather in indoor premises with another person who is not—*
>
> *(i) a member of their household,*
>
> *(ii) their carer, or*
>
> *(iii) a person they are providing care to.*"

Regulation 8(2) gives a non-exhaustive list of what might constitute a 'reasonable excuse'. Some of the examples given are attending a funeral, fulfilling a legal obligation or voting in an election.

Regulation 8(3)(b) explicitly adds, however, that it is not a reasonable excuse to leave, or remain away from, the area in which the person is living to do anything that it would be reasonably practicable for the person to do within the area.

Regulation 8A: Working from Home

Under Regulation 8A, a person must not work out of the home, where it would be reasonably practicable to work from home.

Regulation 8B: Gathering Outdoors

Regulation 8B prohibits any gatherings outdoors except for certain conditions. The first is that the gathering is made up of no more than two households; this differs from the English Regulations that specify that an outdoor gathering of no more than six people is permitted (who might conceivably be from six different households).

Other exceptions include where the gathering is necessary for work purposes, where the gathering is necessary to provide emergency assistance to a person, and where necessary to fulfil a legal obligation.

Regulation 9: Closure of Public Paths and Land

Regulation 9 of the Welsh Regulations applies where the relevant local authority considers that an area of land is liable to large numbers of people congregating or otherwise poses a high risk to the incidence of spread of coronavirus. In that case, the local authority is mandated by Regulation 9 to close the public access or land. It is to remain closed until either the end of the emergency period or until it is no longer deemed necessary to keep it closed.

Regulation 10: Enforcement

Regulation 10 of the Welsh Regulations largely mirrors the rules as to enforcement in the English Regulations.

Regulation 12: Offences and Penalties

The key parts of Regulation 12 state as follows:

"*12.— Offences and penalties*

(1) A person who—

(a) without reasonable excuse, contravenes a requirement in [regulation 4, 5(3C),6, 6A, 7, 8A, 8B or 9(4)]1, or

(b) contravenes a requirement in regulation 8(1),

commits an offence.

(2) A person who obstructs, without reasonable excuse, any person carrying out a function under these Regulations commits an offence.

(3) A person who, without reasonable excuse, contravenes a direction, or fails to comply with an instruction or a prohibition notice, given by a relevant person under regulation 10 commits an offence.

(4) An offence under these Regulations is punishable on summary conviction by a fine.

(5) Section 24 of the Police and Criminal Evidence Act 19843 applies in relation to an offence under this regulation as if the reasons in subsection (5) included—

(a) to maintain public health;

(b) to maintain public order.

(6) If an offence under paragraph (1) committed by a body corporate is proved—

(a) to have been committed with the consent or connivance of an officer of the body, or

> *(b) to be attributable to any neglect on the part of such an officer,*
>
> *the officer (as well as the body corporate) is guilty of the offence and liable to be prosecuted and proceeded against and punished accordingly."*

The remainder of Regulation 12 sets out further clarification and explanatory provisions in relation to the prosecution of a company.

As in the English Regulations, a person will not be guilty of an offence unless they had no reasonable excuse for breaching the relevant Regulations.

Also as in the English Regulations, the offences are triable only summarily, and the maximum penalty is an unspecified fine.

Regulation 13: Fixed Penalty Notices

Regulation 13 of the Welsh Regulations largely mirrors the English provisions as to fixed penalty notices. The key difference is in the amount; in Wales, the fixed penalty notice starts at £60 to be paid within 28 days, which is reduced to £30 if paid within 14 days. The amounts then double for each subsequent notice received, capped at £1920 in the case of the sixth and any subsequent fixed penalty notice received.

Regulation 14: Prosecutions

The Welsh Regulations include a provision as to prosecution that is entirely absent from the English Regulations. Regulation 14 states that no proceedings for an offence under the Welsh Regulations may be brought other than by the Director of Public Prosecutions or any person designated by the Welsh Ministers.

Regulation 15: Expiry

Finally, the Welsh Regulations will expire six months after their coming into force, under Regulation 15. That does not affect the validity of anything done pursuant to the Regulations before they expire. In other words, charges commenced during the life of the Regulations can still continue to be prosecuted once the Regulations expire.

CHAPTER FOUR
HOW COVID-19 IMPACTS CURRENT OFFENCES

This chapter considers the way in which Covid-19 impacts upon existing criminal offences. It focuses on particular offences that have seen a significant increase in reporting and why. It considers what impact this might have on the types of offences we see commonly prosecuted in the courts, and whether there will be changes to the way those cases are treated.

OVERVIEW

It would be no exaggeration to say that the 'lockdown' period changed virtually everybody's way of life. People were staying in their homes more, there were far fewer people on the streets and public transport was at a virtual standstill.

It might stand to reason, then, that certain offences would see a dip in their frequency; for example, there would be far fewer opportunities to pick pockets, and all but the most brazen burglars might be deterred by the idea that entire households were present in their homes for the vast majority of the day.

However, certain types of offences could be susceptible to increase during both the specific lockdown period, and generally under a period of heightened stress and anxiety, like the pandemic. It is important for all those working in the criminal justice system to be alive to the potential ways in which certain offences might be impacted by the climate under Covid-19.

HATE CRIME

In February and March 2020, the news was spreading that a deadly new virus first spotted in China had now extended its reach around the world. It showed no sign of slowing down, let alone stopping. As the weeks continued, it became ever clear that the country was marching towards measures of quarantine and containment that were unprecedented in modern times. At the same time, the Metropolitan Police recorded 166 verbal, online and physical attacks in February and March where the officer reported the ethnic appearance of the victim as 'oriental'. This was an increase of 66 incidents compared to the same period last year[1].

Unfortunately, this is not a great surprise when we look at even our relatively recent history. It seems that when people are facing a large and terrifying threat, they seek to pin responsibility on something or someone that they can see and touch. So it is that in the aftermath of the 9/11 attacks, and again in the aftermath of the 7/7 attacks in the United Kingdom, there were wide ranging reports of increased victimisation of those who were (or were perceived to be) Muslim.

The criminal law provides a structure of offences and sentencing powers to tackle hate crime in the criminal courts. Broadly speaking, the criminal law's approach can be said to be split between: a) offences of which an essential element is the hate crime component (e.g. racially aggravated assault); b) all other offences, which will be subject to a sentencing uplift if the Court considers that the hate crime component is proven.

---

1 As provided to the Financial Times in response to a Freedom of Information Request, see https://www.ft.com/content/52e7062b-0cb2-448a-b944-05b3025d4542, last accessed on 27 June 2020.

The specific hate crime offences are mostly found in the Crime and Disorder Act 1998 and the Public Order Act 1986. If the crime with which you are dealing is not a specific hate crime offence, then it will be subject to the sentencing uplift. The provisions as to sentencing uplift are found in sections 145 and 146 of the Criminal Justice Act 2003.

The current characteristics that are protected under the legislation dealing with hate crime are race, religion, sexual orientation, disability and transgender identity. 'Race' (specifically, in relation to people of East Asian, or perceived East Asian, ethnicity) seems likely to be the characteristic most at risk of seeing a spike in criminal offences due to the coronavirus pandemic.

DOMESTIC ABUSE

For many of us, the key concern in dealing with 'lockdown' was how to organise working from home or cope with reduction in income, how to keep young members of the family entertained and how to maintain a social life whilst respecting social distancing. For those living in the cloud of an abusive relationship, however, it has become apparent that it is no exaggeration to say that 'lockdown' was tantamount to a prison sentence. When we stop to consider this, it seems all too obvious. Not only would those being subject to abuse now be confined in one place with their abuser, but they were living in the increasingly anxious climate of the pandemic. For some time, it has been well documented that financial concerns, job losses and other external stresses can exacerbate the likelihood of domestic abuse. There were then, added to the mix, restrictions on why and how often people can leave the home. That, coupled with the likely difficulty in some cases of finding space to make a private telephone call when stuck in quarantine, slashed the opportunities those abused had to seek help.

The data supports this conclusion. A Home Affairs Select Committee report published on 27 April 2020 cited evidence from the national domestic abuse charity Refuge, indicating that calls to its helpline were 49% higher in the week prior to 15 April 2020 than the average prior to the pandemic[2].

Those of us working in the criminal justice system should, then, be aware that there may be a peak in domestic abuse cases before the courts. We should familiarise ourselves with the law governing incidents of domestic abuse.

Specific offences are enshrined in different parts of the criminal law. Physical and sexual assaults are provided for through numerous pieces of legislation, designed to deal with those offences in a domestic and non-domestic context. The last decade, though, saw a deeper understanding of the fact that domestic abuse can manifest itself in numerous ways years before the first fist is raised. So it was that section 76 of the Serious Crime Act 2015 created the offence of 'controlling and coercive behaviour'. That offence is committed where the offender engages in continuous or repeated conduct, that is controlling and coercive, towards a person with whom they are intimately connected, on whom the behaviour has a serious effect and the offender knows (or ought to know) that the behaviour has a serious effect.

This offence, then, covers not only actual violence but threats of violence, controlling the social behaviour of someone, financial control,

---

2 See report at https://publications.parliament.uk/pa/cm5801/cmselect/cmhaff/321/32105.htm, last accessed on 27 June 2020.

emotional and mental abuse – perhaps, generally, it could be said to encompass all behaviour that causes the person at whom it is targeted to 'walk on eggshells', living in a state of mental and emotional subjugation.

Note also that at the time of writing, the Domestic Abuse Bill is making its way through Parliament. That Bill includes a statutory definition of domestic abuse, and provides specific powers in relation to how it is treated in the courts.

It remains to be seen whether the courts will deal any differently with cases of domestic abuse committed during the pandemic and, particularly, during lockdown period. For example, it could reasonably be argued that the offences are significantly aggravated by the fact that the country was in lockdown at the time of the offence. Seeking assistance to escape your abuser should, undoubtedly, constitute a 'reasonable excuse' for breaching the Regulations. However, it must not be forgotten that the prevailing public message – during lockdown in particular - was that to stay elsewhere than at home would be to seriously risk your health, and that of any children you chose to take with you. Hotels, B&Bs and the like were not operating for the general public. To stay with family members might bring added worry to the abused person that they could be transmitting something to their family, or catch something in turn. Turning to a refuge would be the only option left; that would not necessarily allay concerns about the risks of catching Covid-19 or, indeed, children catching the disease. Taking all that into account, it may well be arguable that the offence was aggravated by the fact that the abuser knew that his victim's options for seeking help and escape were severely limited, both by practical means and by the firm, national message to 'stay where you are'.

REVENGE PORN

Linked in some ways to domestic abuse, we may expect to see increased incidents of 'revenge porn'. This is the offence of publicising intimate images of others without their consent.

The offence is found in section 33 of the Criminal Justice and Courts Act 2015. It is an offence to disclose private sexual photographs or films without the consent of an individual who appears in them and with intent to cause that individual distress. It is triable either way, and the maximum sentence that can be imposed is two years' imprisonment.

There are at least two reasons why we might see a rise in 'revenge porn' cases. First, people spending more time at home are likely spending more time online. Many businesses that can work online are encouraging their employees to work from home. The closure of shops means that people turn to online shopping. People access training and lectures through webinars and online conferencing. During 'lockdown' in particular, we became a nation of people interacting with the outside world almost entirely through our computers.

Secondly, there is the element of control. 'Revenge porn' can be seen as a facet of domestic abuse; it is a way of causing extreme distress to someone, embarrassing them, blackmailing them and otherwise getting their attention. All those are forms of control. A person may not be living with their abuser; they may live separately, or the relationship may have ended. Where the abuser can no longer physically travel to access and harass their victim, 'revenge porn' is a way of doing so online. Their victim can ignore repeated text messages and telephone calls; it may be virtually impossible to ignore the sharing of intimate images of themselves with the World Wide Web.

Again, it may be arguable that the context aggravates any 'revenge porn' offence committed during lockdown. After all, if most people are using the Internet most of the time, the victim might reasonably fear that more people will have viewed the images before he or she has had a chance to get them removed. Linked to that is the possibility that the offender was aware of their greater viewing figures at this time. It is an argument that would need to be developed and considered in the context of the facts of each individual case, but it may well be one worth exploring.

ONLINE FRAUD

I have referred to the increased numbers of people using the Internet for social interaction, work and shopping. This includes people who might not have relied upon the Internet heavily before, such as members of the elderly community. In addition, there was a period around the start of lockdown where there were wide-ranging reports about a dearth of certain products, such as toilet roll and hand sanitiser. When they were sold out of shops, the next logical place to look was the Internet. Added to all that, little was known or revealed in terms of the medical aspects of Covid-19 and whether certain medicines or vitamins might help raise immunity. Conditions were ripe for online fraud.

This logic is borne out by the statistics. The City of London Police reported a 400% increase in reports of online fraud in March 2020[3]. Widely reported examples have included bogus sites offering hand sanitiser, face masks and similar protective products, phishing emails

3 As reported in the Financial Times, at https://www.ft.com/content/9800243b-9d2e-4b98-a6fd-bdc498da3ef9, last accessed on 27 June 2020.

sending a link to a malicious attachment designed to steal people's details and, perhaps most cruelly, telephone calls telling the recipient that they have been in contact with an infected person and will receive a testing kit – if they just provide their bank details.

Of course, the particular difficulty with online fraud is prosecuting those responsible. First, the Internet transcends physical boundaries; it is perfectly feasible that the perpetrator of a fraud in the United Kingdom is seated in a foreign jurisdiction many thousands of miles away. Even if they are identified, the thorny and protracted process of international legal relations will mean that they are unlikely to face the criminal courts in the UK for some time, if at all.

Secondly, those skilled in the anatomy of the Internet may have sophisticated measures for hiding their identity. It may be that, as those investigating them start on their trail, they are able to disappear with little trace, in a flash of the time it would take them to do so physically. This is not even the sort of crime where the victim has face to face contact with the fraudster and can assist the police in identifying the offender. The victim may not even know whether they are dealing with one person or a network of people, male or female.

It will remain to be seen, then, whether our criminal courts see any immediate spike in prosecutions for online fraud. Given the issues that I have touched upon above, it may be that we do not see such prosecutions for a few years to come.

CORPORATE MANSLAUGHTER AND GROSS NEGLIGENCE MANSLAUGHTER

Section 1 of the Corporate Manslaughter and the Corporate Homicide Act 2007 created the offence of Corporate Manslaughter. Under that provision, an organisation is guilty of an offence if the way in which its activities are managed and organised: (a) caused a death; and (b) amounts to a gross breach of the relevant duty of care owed by the organisation to the deceased.

The provision only applies to certain organisations, defined by the Act. That includes limited companies and partnerships.

During the pandemic period, certain organisations have continued to operate. Those include organisations responsible for delivery services, or takeaway food and drink. It is a given that people continuing to work in those organisations will need greater protections than those who remain isolated in their homes. If there were a situation where a company had failed to put into place significant measures to mitigate risk to its employees, and deaths followed, it is quite possible that such a company could face a prosecution for Corporate Manslaughter. The threshold is a high one though; the breach of the duty of care must be '*gross*'.

Similarly, those individuals owing a duty of care to others (e.g. doctors) face a difficult task. They continue to provide medical assistance, whilst battling a disease that is novel and deadly. The case of *R v Adomako* (1995) 1 AC 171 set out the ingredients of the offence of gross negligence manslaughter as follows:

> "*On this basis, in my opinion the ordinary principles of negligence apply to ascertain whether or not the defendant has been in breach of a duty of care towards the victim who has died. If such breach*

of duty is established the next question is whether that breach of duty caused the death of the victim. If so, the jury must go on to consider whether that breach of duty should be characterised as gross negligence and therefore as a crime."

Again, the standard of negligence is high; it must be "*gross*'. Nevertheless, it is possible that a person such as a medical professional whose standards of care fell beyond those acceptable and which caused the death might find themselves in Court facing a charge of gross negligence manslaughter for actions that resulted in a person succumbing to Covid-19 where they might otherwise have not.

There have been no widely reported instances of either offence in relation to deaths from Covid-19 at the time of writing. A detailed analysis of both is beyond the scope of this Essential Guide. Nevertheless, it is useful to be aware of their existence, and the possibility that they might rear their heads as the pandemic continues.

PART TWO

THE IMPACT OF COVID-19 ON THE CRIMINAL COURT SYSTEM

CHAPTER FIVE
MAKING JUSTICE VIRTUAL – PRE AND POST TRIAL HEARINGS

This chapter considers the use of virtual hearings to replace physical hearings during the pandemic. It focuses on pre and post-trial hearings, as trials have been dealt with differently, and so are addressed separately in Chapter 4. This chapter looks at the law and practice of virtual hearings during the pandemic, and considers whether virtual hearings might have a place in the long term.

OVERVIEW

When lockdown was announced on 23 March 2020, the criminal courts faced an unprecedented situation: overnight, the courts were unfit for purpose, without breaching the governmental guidance and putting their users at risk. Any practitioner who has spent time in the criminal courts pre-lockdown can see why. The criminal courts are busy, often fast-paced environments. From the moment that a practitioner enters the court building, they and their possessions are searched by security, they are surrounded by other people and they necessarily need to speak with several people in a short period of time. The robing rooms for advocates are of varying sizes; it is not a mistake to say that few criminal courts in England and Wales have robing rooms that facilitate social distancing without strict rules as to entry being put in place.

The courtrooms themselves may often be full of advocates who are either being heard at the time, or are waiting in the rows of benches behind for their hearing to be called on. Those defendants in custody are brought in vans to be deposited in a set of one-person cells that are, often, underground in windowless parts of the building. Advocates holding conferences with those clients will usually be placed opposite their clients in a small room designed to accommodate two people relatively comfortably, or to squeeze in three. Maintaining a distance of over a metre is, therefore, generally unworkable.

This is even more so when conducting a trial. Then, at least 18 people (Judge, jury, two advocates, defendant and two members of court staff) will be in the courtroom at any one time. The jurors will be sitting in a group of twelve, wedged into a jury box alongside each other. Usually they will be asked to share important documents between themselves in pairs.

The immediate solution, then, was to close the courts on 24 March 2020 and promptly list all non-trial hearings virtually. Such a wide-scale transfer of cases to the virtual forum was unprecedented. It should be remembered, though, that there were already provisions in place to conduct telephone or video hearings. The Criminal Practice Direction Amendment Order [2017] EWCA Crim 30 set out changes to the Criminal Practice Directions to allow live link or telephone hearings to be conducted where in the interests of justice to do so. Thus the concept was not completely alien to the criminal court system. However, the use of such facilities on such a widespread scale was alien; with the rapid transition to those facilities, it followed that there was inevitably going to be disruption. The area of the criminal justice system that has arguably faced the most disruption is trials. They now face an immense backlog, and no universally satisfactory solution has been proposed to ease that. They will be discussed further in Chapter 4. However, virtual hearings in all other areas have their benefits and disadvantages, and these will be discussed below.

VIRTUAL HEARINGS DURING THE PANDEMIC: THE LAW

Although there already existed provisions in the Criminal Procedure Rules for telephone and live-link hearings, the Coronavirus Act 2020 sets out specific provisions in its Schedules 23 to 26. Those Schedules amend existing legislation to expand the powers of the courts to require or allow participation in hearings virtually.

Schedule 23 of the Coronavirus Act 2020 deals with criminal proceedings (e.g. trial, appeals). It amends section 51 of the Criminal Justice Act 2003, to allow that a person may take part in 'eligible criminal proceedings' via a live audio link or a live video link, if the court directs. 'Eligible criminal proceedings' includes appeals to the Crown Court and any trial in the Crown Court. The Court may not give such a direction unless satisfied that it is in the interests of justice for the person concerned to take part in the proceedings in accordance with the directions, the parties have the opportunity to make representations and the relevant youth offending team (if relevant) has the opportunity to make representations.

Paragraph 4 of that Schedule clarifies that a person required to attend proceedings who attends under a section 51 direction (i.e. virtually) is to be treated as complying with the requirement to attend.

Schedule 24 to the Coronavirus Act 2020 deals with live links in other criminal hearings – i.e. preliminary, sentencing and enforcement hearings. It amends the Crime and Disorder Act 1998 ("the 1998 Act"). By paragraph 3 of Schedule 24, section 57B of the 1998 Act is amended so as to allow the court to direct or permit a person to take part in a preliminary hearing through a live audio or video link. This is subject to the requirement that the Court must be satisfied it is in the interests to do so, the parties have had the opportunity to make representations and the relevant youth offending team (if appropriate) has had the opportunity to make representations.

Paragraph 4 of Schedule 24 to the Coronavirus Act 2020 provides for the use of live link in sentencing hearings, and amends section 57E of the 1998 Act. Before the Coronavirus Act 2002, section 57E only allowed the Court to order live links for sentencing hearings where the defendant was in custody. However, now, the Court may require or permit a person to take part in a sentencing hearing through a live audio or video link. The same requirements apply as under the amendments made by paragraph 3 – the Court must be satisfied that it is in the interests of justice to order the link, and the parties and youth offending team must have the opportunity to make representations.

Paragraph 5 of Schedule 24 to the Coronavirus Act 2020 provides for the use of live link in enforcement hearings – i.e. hearings to enforce unpaid confiscation orders. It amends section 57F of the 1998 Act. Again, the Court may require or permit a person to take part in an enforcement hearing through live audio or video link. The same requirements apply as to ensuring that it is in the interests of justice, and that the parties and youth offending team have the opportunity to make representations.

Note, however, that where a person attends an enforcement hearing via audio link only, the Court may not: a) impose imprisonment or detention in default of payment of a sum or financial penalty; or b) deal with a person for contempt of court. If there is the possibility of either of those matters arising, then, it would be advisable for the Court to list the enforcement hearing via video link.

Paragraph 6 clarifies that a person attending a hearing virtually, in accordance with the provisions above, is to be treated as complying with the requirement to attend court. A hearing conducted wholly as an audio or video hearing is to be regarded as taking place at the location where the member of members of the court take part in the hearing. So it is that where a virtual hearing has a Judge and court staff seated at a Crown Court, the prosecution advocated seated in their home and defence advocate seated at their home, the hearing will be treated as taking place at the Crown Court that houses the members of the court.

Paragraph 7 inserts a new Schedule 3A into the 1998 Act. This sets out various prohibitions and limitations on the use of live links. Of most note in relation to preliminary hearings are the following points. The accused may not participate over a solely audio link in preliminary hearings where: a) they are to give evidence; b) the preliminary hearing is a contested bail hearing; c) the accused is being dealt with for contempt of court; d) they are entering a guilty plea. Fitness to plead hearings may not be conducted wholly as a video hearing, and the accused may not take part in the hearing through a live audio link (Part 1 of Schedule 3A to the 1998 Act).

Of most note in relation to sentencing hearings is the fact that the offender may not take part in a sentencing hearing through a live audio link. It follows that all sentencing hearings should be listed as video link hearings (Part 2 of Schedule 3A to the 1998 Act).

Of most note in relation to enforcement hearings are the following points: a) the person liable to pay the relevant sum may not give evidence over an audio link; b) if the Court is minded to impose imprisonment or detention on a person in default of payment of a sum or financial penalty, then the liable person cannot take part through a live audio link; c) if the Court is minded to deal with a person for contempt of court, then that person may not take part through a live audio link. Where any of these matters are likely to arise, then, the virtual hearing should be schedule to take place via video link.

Schedule 25 of the Coronavirus Act 2020 makes amendment to the Courts Act 2003 to set out provisions for public participation in virtual proceedings. Schedule 25 inserts new sections 85A to 85D into the Courts Act 2003. The key points to note are as follows. The Court may direct that proceedings taking place wholly by audio or video link are to be broadcast to allow access to members of the public. The Court may also direct that a recording of proceedings is to be made to keep a record of those proceedings. It is, though, an offence for a person to make or attempt to make an unauthorised recording or transmission of the hearing. This ensures, then, that the prohibitions on members of the public recording in-person court proceedings are expanded to include virtual proceedings.

Finally, schedule 26 of the Coronavirus Act 2020 makes amendments to the Magistrates' Courts Act 1980 to set out provisions for the use of live links in certain Magistrates' Court proceedings. The main points to note are as follows. Where a person is appealing against a requirement or restriction imposed on potentially infected persons, the proceedings are to be conducted wholly as video proceedings unless the court directs otherwise. This makes sense when we consider that, by definition, the person appealing will have been considered by someone to be potentially infectious – and so the presumption should be that they are able to participate in the hearing whilst remaining in isolation.

As with preceding provisions relating to the Crown Court, a person who takes part in the proceedings through an audio or video live link is to be treated as complying with any requirement to attend. Again, as with preceding provisions, the Court may direct that the proceedings are to be broadcast to members of the public, but it remains an offence to make or transmit an unauthorised recording.

VIRTUAL HEARINGS DURING THE PANDEMIC: PRACTICAL GUIDANCE

At the time of writing, there are at least three virtual platforms that are being used in the criminal courts. Each has its own advantages and disadvantages; each court seems to have settled on one of those as their platform of choice. It is beyond the scope of this book – and of my technical knowledge – to embark on a detailed comparison study of the different virtual platforms. However, plainly it would be most desirable to have one unified platform with the appropriate features for use in a court.

It is difficult, given the different court platforms and approaches, to set out a practical roadmap for the practitioner taking part in a virtual hearing. However, there are some tips that are of general application, and may be useful to the practitioner:

- If the hearing is likely to involve detailed or complicated issues, it would be good practice to upload submissions in a written document sufficiently in advance of the hearing;
- Upload your name, details of who you represent and professional contact details onto a widely shared comment before the hearing. This will ensure not only that the representative of the other side can contact you if needed, but that the court has an easy reference to contact you if there are technical problems;

- In terms of dress, there is no requirement to wear robes. However, aside from that, appropriate court dress is required i.e. dark suits, white shirt or blouse;
- Be ready to log into the system around 15 minutes before the hearing. This will ensure that you are not delayed by any technical problems or difficulties logging in, and allow liaison between advocates;
- Have your notes on a separate device, or in hard copy. This is a small tip, and subject to personal preference, but it would avoid you clicking between the video platform and other screens on the laptop;
- Ensure that you are in a room that is quiet, allows you a relatively neutral background and has good internet connection;
- When you are not talking, it may be a good idea to put yourself on 'mute'. This prevents background noise from your surroundings interrupting other participants in the case.

THE FUTURE OF VIRTUAL HEARINGS

The Criminal Courts have been hauled into the virtual world with sudden force. However, now that we have the system in place and running, the question arises: what is the future of virtual hearings?

There are some clear advantages to continuing to hold non-trial hearings by audio or video link.

First, having a video hearing can save a significant amount of time. Any junior barrister will know all too well the heart-sinking moment they receive a call at 5p.m. to tell them that they will be in a city three hours' travel time away first thing in the morning. All too often, the hearing they will be travelling across the country to attend will last no longer than fifteen minutes. Thus, the barrister has lost an entire day travelling to and from a court for fifteen minutes of advocacy time. A virtual hearing immediately dispels that problem.

Secondly, and linked, the virtual hearing can save a significant amount of money for those appearing in it. We can illustrate this by returning to the same situation of the junior barrister called to attend a court some three hours away for a short hearing. The barrister travelling by train or by car will likely spend a significant amount of money on train or petrol costs. That cost will be only mildly offset by the fees they receive for the hearing, which can easily amount to only a quarter of the amount that they have shelled out to attend. It is not uncommon, then, for barristers to make a loss on any given day. This problem is all the more keenly felt by those at the start of their careers, for whom covering short hearings in more senior barristers' cases is often their 'bread and butter' income. It is not uncommon for those at the bottom end of the profession to amass debts in the forms of loans and credit cards, whilst running around the country to act in poorly paid hearings.

Thirdly, virtual hearings make it easier for an advocate to conduct several hearings a day. They will not be constrained by the requirement that each hearing be within easy travelling distance or in the same court. A barrister could conduct one hearing in Isleworth Crown Court in the morning, and another in Birmingham Crown Court at midday, without the pressure and stress of making virtually impossible travel times. This links to the points above. Not only does it reduce the time wasted in travelling, but it also impacts on finances. The barrister will not be spending money to attend the hearing, and will be able to earn two or three times as much as they might be able to otherwise, by conducting two or three hearings in a day.

Fourthly, virtual hearings might make it easier for the barrister instructed on the trial to attend preliminary or sentencing hearings in their own cases. When hearings are all conducted in person, the barrister instructed on a trial might often find themselves in the undesirable position of being unable to attend preliminary hearings as they are requested in another court, on a hearing that must take priority. Where there are virtual hearings, it could be possible for counsel instructed on a trial to attend the preliminary hearing virtually, whilst then being able to attend the other hearing at which they are required, either virtually or in person.

There are, though, some disadvantages to holding virtual hearings.

The first is the state of technology. In order for virtual hearings to be effective, the technology must be sophisticated, secure and able to support different functions. For example, at the moment, there is little ability to hold a pre-hearing conference with a client. Virtual hearings often work through allowing all parties into one virtual 'room'. This is not conducive to allowing defence counsel to have a private, virtual conference with their client. In order for things to progress satisfactorily, there would need to be a facility to set up another, secure virtual 'room' which the client and defence counsel would access before the hearing, at an appointed time, in order to hold a conference.

In terms of technology, it will also be most desirable to establish and implement one virtual system that is used universally in England and Wales. That system can then be tailored towards the needs of the criminal court system. For example, it will need to be able to deal with the delays that often happen in hearings (where a previous hearing overruns, for example), so cannot be tied to specific times of use. There should be a system to 'lock' a hearing, or to provide different virtual 'rooms' for each case, so that people do not accidentally enter the hearing that takes place before theirs. Once there is one virtual courts platform, there can then be a unified, coherent approach. There will need to be a national training package rolled out so that all users are familiar with the system. At the time of writing, there is a tailored courts platform newly in place, but it remains to be seen whether it will in fact be rolled out across every court centre, and it is too early to make a reliable assessment of its efficacy in this book.

Secondly, there are advantages to being face to face in a hearing. The primary, and most obvious perhaps, is where a person needs to give evidence. Trials are dealt with separately in the next chapter; but there are other hearings where a person may give evidence. For example, a contested confiscation hearing will require evidence to be given. There may be character witnesses called at a sentencing hearing. If a person appears to give evidence virtually, then arguably some of the solemnity of the courtroom is lost. There is much to be said in terms of emphasising the seriousness of proceedings by the witness attending at the court building, with all the formalities that involves, and taking the oath in person.

There is also the advantage of being able to deal with last-minute issues if appearing in person. For example, a document may be handed to the advocate at the last minute, to present to the Judge. The defendant may wish to change instructions during the hearing or have a word with their advocate. Those are all matters that are made more difficult in virtual hearings. Last-minute documents can be uploaded onto the digital case system in the crown courts; the magistrates' courts operate no such digital case system, and it is unclear how such a situation could be smoothly dealt with. If the client in a virtual hearing wishes to have a word with their advocate, it is unclear how this could be affected in an efficient manner, whilst respecting legal privilege and confidentiality. The way to address this would be to make improvements to the technology. The provision of a private 'room' for an advocate and their client might help deal with in-hearing instructions. A provision for online document sharing would help deal with documents to be handed to the Bench in the Magistrates' Court.

THE BEST SOLUTION?

Overall, it seems that with some changes to the technical systems to iron out the issues set out above, virtual hearings can and should form a more permanent part of the criminal justice system. It is simply a waste of money, time and efficiency to require practitioners to travel hundreds of miles for short hearings, when they can be heard remotely. Not only will this save time and expense for those appearing in the hearings, but can also open space in Court buildings for more of those cases that must be heard in person to be so heard (such as trials, or other cases involving witnesses). After all, the Judge could conceivably conduct the hearing in Chambers, with all others appearing remotely, thus freeing up an entire courtroom.

Of course, it is rare that a 'one size fits all' approach works in the criminal justice system; there will always be cases where issues unique to that case mean it is more desirable that all parties attend in person. I would suggest, though, that this can be adequately catered for by having a presumption that a pre-trial or post-trial hearing will be virtual (perhaps aside from those hearings where live witnesses are required, such as a contested confiscation hearing or an appeal in the Crown Court), unless either the Judge or one or more parties to the hearing consider that it should not be. A brief and pointed paper application could then be made for the hearing to be in person if needed. This will avoid the listing in person of relatively straightforward hearings to enter pleas, set dates for future hearings, make a decision as to sentence or to make brief legal arguments – and bring with it multiple advantages for all in terms of time, space and money.

CHAPTER SIX
THE JURY QUESTION

This chapter considers the question of how to hear jury trials during the pandemic. It looks at alternatives to the traditional trial by jury system, and their relative advantages and disadvantages.

OVERVIEW

Chapter Three discussed virtual hearings – excluding trials. At the time of writing, the vast majority of trials have been adjourned to a later date. The latest HMCTS figures suggested that over 40,000 trials have been adjourned during the time of the lockdown. That is an astounding figure, and conjures fears of an insurmountable backlog.

What, then, should be done? Trials present their own unique array of problems that do not arise in short hearings. First, the defendant should be able to fully participate in the trial. That not only means the right to give evidence, but to be able to hear and see all the evidence against him, to instruct his advocate as to the questioning of witnesses and arguments to be put forward on his behalf. In order to give effect to that on a virtual platform, a sophisticated and reliable technological system would be required.

Secondly, there is the question of the jury. Any defendant being tried in the Crown Court has the right to be tried by a jury of 12 of his peers. Before the pandemic, jurors sat together in the jury box, side by side, sharing documents between them. Transferring this to a virtual or a socially distanced platform is not a straightforward matter.

Thirdly, there is the issue of witnesses giving evidence. One of the key advantages of having a witness give live evidence is allowing the jury to observe their mannerisms in person. It is for that reason that the witness will give evidence in person in court, unless certain specified exceptions apply (such as the witness being vulnerable, or a child). If a witness were to give evidence over a virtual platform, there is the risk that something would be lost in the ability to observe their mannerisms in full, and reach an assessment of that.

Having said all of that, the option to adjourn jury trials until a date in the future when the restrictions may be reduced significantly is simply not tenable. At the time of writing, there is no clear indication of when the country might return to a pre-pandemic climate. With every day that the restrictions continue, the backlog of trials continue. We need to avoid the situation where we return to the crown court only to find that trials are habitually being delayed by several years. There is also the question of the sustainability of a practice for the criminal practitioner. As noted above, the short hearings are not the ones that provide a sustainable income. Advocates often rely on trials to keep their income healthy. Out of that fee, they must pay Chambers expenses, home expenses, travel expenses, tax, VAT and any other outgoings. Should those advocates be faced with a year, or longer, of no trial work, we should not be surprised if we see many struggling to keep up with their financial obligations.

There are some options to revive Crown Court trials, which have received varying levels of support. I shall consider below the following four options:

i. Reducing or Dispensing of the Jury (trying Crown Court cases by a Judge or a Panel of three);

ii. Socially Distanced Trials, using more than one courtroom;

iii. Virtual Trials;

iv. Reconstituted Buildings – often referred to as 'Nightingale' Courts.

REDUCING OR DISPENSING OF THE JURY

One of the options being mooted is either reducing the number of jurors or dispensing of the jury altogether. Proponents of this option point to measures taken during World War Two. In World War Two, however, the numbers of jurors needed to try a case was reduced.

Reducing the number of jurors would not, when scrutinised, actually be a satisfactory compromise – to effectively maintain social distancing, the number of jurors would have to be greatly slashed. In World War Two, this was not an issue: the enemy was not one that required all the public to maintain at least one metre distance from each other. The jury box would not enable even six people to socially distance sufficiently. In order to allow one metre distance between jury members in the jury box, their numbers would have to be reduced still further – raising the question: will a jury of three really represent a sufficient cross-section of society? Alternatively, they would have to be placed in another courtroom where they could be socially distanced from each other and watch proceedings remotely. In the latter case, then there is no reason why twelve members could not be retained.

Perhaps it is for these reasons that the option to dispense of the jury altogether receives more focus. On the one hand, there are some obvious, practical advantages. The first is that it would require far fewer people in the courtroom: rather than at least 18 people being in a courtroom (Judge, jury, two advocates, defendant and two members of court staff), there would only need to be about six. Days where witnesses are not required might be held remotely. This would then mean that trials could resume much more quickly. At the time of writing, court centres are slowly experimenting with opening for short hearings, where they are able to ensure that advocates can socially distance from each other and appropriate cleaning can take place. There would seem to be no reason why a Judge only trial could not resume just as quickly.

However, those who are fiercely opposed to the idea point to the Centuries' old right of a defendant to be tried by a jury of his peers. Criminal cases involve human emotions and human issues. Twelve men and women can bring their own, unique experiences to a case, untainted by the years of experience dealing with criminal cases that a legal tribunal has. There is, also, safety in numbers, in terms of reaching a truly fair decision on the facts. If two heads are better than one, then twelve heads are undoubtedly better than two.

Furthermore, there is a great advantage in keeping the tribunal of fact and the tribunal of law separate. Under the current jury system, the jury is not present when legal decisions as to admissibility and the like are made. Therefore, the jury is able to assess the factual matrix without having any knowledge of evidence that is not presented before them by virtue of being ruled legally inadmissible. Replacing this with a Judge only trial, or a trial constituted of a Judge and two Magistrates, would remove that barrier.

Finally, some defendants may feel concern that the Judge (or Panel of Judge and Magistrates) is 'out of touch' with their issues, compared to a jury of their peers. The Judiciary is still drawn overwhelmingly from white males of a certain social background. They are generally of a certain mature age. The jury pool will generally be drawn from a wider range of backgrounds, ages, gender and sexual orientation. Overall the jury is likely to have at least some members who will closely understand the particular issues the defendant might have faced.

There is a third alternative to either retaining or dispensing of the jury. That is to adopt a system similar to that found in Canada, and give the defendant the right to elect trial by Judge alone. Effectively, the defendant may avail himself of his right to be tried by his peers, but has the power to dispense of that right should he wish.

Some practitioners may wonder why a defendant would prefer to be tried by one Judge alone (or a Judge and two Magistrates), when he could be tried by twelve of his peers. There are some reasons why a defendant might choose to elect trial by Judge alone. One is where the case involves highly emotive issues. For example, cases involving sexual abuse of children or extreme violence will usually invoke instinctive feelings of revulsion. The defendant may wish to remove the possibility of a jury being overpowered by emotion, and instead rely upon a Judge, who has years of professional experience in putting emotion to one side when the situation demands it.

Another example may be where the case revolves around a legal issue, or examination of experts – such as in a case where the issue is whether the defendant is guilty of murder or manslaughter. In such a situation, the defendant may prefer to place his arguments before a Judge who is an expert in the law, rather than twelve people with significantly less legal experience.

At first glance, allowing the defendant to choose may seem a happy compromise. However, I consider it a wholly undesirable option in the current circumstances. The reason is that it is no secret that trials by jury are severely backlogged. By contrast, a trial by Judge alone could be heard significantly sooner. If, in the current circumstances, we allow the defendant the chance to elect trial by Judge alone, we run the very real risk that the defendant feels that he must choose trial by Judge alone, or else risk waiting a significant time for his trial to be resolved. It will thus be virtually impossible to know whether the defendant's decision was the result of consideration of all the advantages of each – or whether it was based purely on the desire to get the trial over with quickly. No matter what the practical circumstances, we cannot risk the defendant making a choice for any reason other than that it is what he considers best for his defence.

SOCIALLY DISTANCED TRIALS USING MORE THAN ONE COURTROOM

Another option mooted has been holding full jury trials, but maintaining social distance standards. The hurdle to rolling this out across the country has been the layout of the courtrooms themselves. With few exceptions, many courtrooms are too small to be able to fit all 18 or so people needed for a trial into one room whilst maintaining at least one metre distance between them all. For that reason, some Courts have experimented with a system of using two or three courtrooms at a time, for one trial. Generally, the jury will be socially distanced in one courtroom whilst the advocates and witnesses will be in another. The jury will be watching the proceedings by means of video link.

The advantages of this are that it would enable us to retain the trial by jury system, whilst also mitigating the risks to anybody's health. The jury will physically be in a courtroom (rather than, say, at home attending over a virtual platform) and so the solemnity of proceedings will be preserved. This system does allow trials to start again, and so work towards clearing the backlog.

However, there are problems with this solution. It is true that it would allow trials to start again, but the necessity for each trial to use at least two courtrooms means that the number of trials that can be listed is slashed by at least half. Some Crown Courts are lucky to have 15 or more courtrooms. Others, though, have far fewer. Equally, the Crown Court would need to ensure that its jury room and witness room were large enough to accommodate those attending as jurors or witnesses whilst maintaining social distancing. Given all the practical constraints, it is not yet clear whether the number of trials that could be heard in this way would make any significant dent on the backlog overall.

VIRTUAL TRIALS

Another option is to hold trials via a virtual platform, the way that other hearings have been conducted. This option does have advantages over the two options previously considered. It would remove the need to dispense of a jury, as the first option requires. A greater number of trials could be held than under the second option, where the volume of trials that can be heard is limited by the venue's constraints. Therefore, virtual trials have the potential to make serious inroad into the backlog

However, there are problems with this option. First, it is questionable as to whether the technology currently available is appropriate for holding a trial. There needs to be facility to exclude the jury when legal discussion is taking place, and ensure that no jury member accidentally or deliberately remains in the room. The technology must be able to accommodate 12 jurors, the Judge, court staff, advocates and the defendant(s), without reducing people to thumbnails on the screen. The jury will need to be able to see the witnesses in order to evaluate them. There will need to be provision for special measures. For example, some witnesses give evidence from behind a physical screen; with careful placement of the screen, they are hidden from all but the advocates, the Judge and the jury. It is unclear how that could transfer to an online platform, which will include the defendant and may be broadcast to the public.

Secondly, there is arguably an element of solemnity that is lost when people are taken out of a courtroom setting and attend virtually. One of the arguments still put forward for maintaining court dress, and certain other customs, is to preserve the serious nature of proceedings. That is not simply for show; but also to ensure that people take their obligations to the court seriously. The oath taken by jurors and by witnesses is more than a few words read from a laminated piece of paper; it is an obligation to abide by the terms of the oath. It is quite possible that some of the seriousness of that would be lost were the surroundings to be removed.

Thirdly, there is the problem touched upon above, of the need for the jury to assess a witness. When a witness gives live evidence, she does more than impress her words upon the jury. The way that she responds to questioning, what she looks at, whether she fidgets, how she sits or stands – all of these are factors that the jury will observe when they are determining whether they find the witness credible. Witnesses can be the cornerstone of a case. Any dilution of the jury's ability to evaluate a witness's credibility should therefore be made with the utmost caution.

RECONSTITUTED BUILDINGS: 'NIGHTINGALE COURTS'

Finally, an option that is being considered is the so-called 'Nightingale Court'. This essentially refers to the option of opening buildings that were not built for court purposes, and using them as reconstituted courts. At the time of writing, they are colloquially referred to as 'Nightingale Courts' – and so I shall refer to them in that way in this section.

Advantages of the 'Nightingale Courts' are that, if suitably large venues are used, it would be possible to have more socially distanced trials. These buildings could be selected for their space and structure. We would not, then, be faced with the problems of having a Court building that simply cannot accommodate large numbers of socially distanced people. It would follow that trials could start again, without the need for dispensing of the jury. If the right building is chosen, the solemnity of the occasion can be preserved.

However, on the other hand, the question is whether 'Nightingale Courts' would actually make a real dent to the backlog. It is unclear how many buildings are both available and suitable for such use. The buildings would need to have facility to implement appropriate security measures, be set up in such a way as to ensure that the jury, witnesses, defendant, lawyers, court staff and Judge can be kept separate where appropriate. It is essential, for example, that the jury have separate facilities than the advocates and defendant, to avoid any contamination. It is also essential that witnesses are kept separate from both the jury and the defendant.

In theory, the 'Nightingale Court' system might be a satisfactory solution. It will allow us to keep jury trials and mitigate any health risks. However, all will depend on just how practical the 'Nightingale Court' option is – just how many buildings are available and suitable, and how much inroad they can realistically make on the backlog.

Of course, there are some buildings that are both available and suitable: between 2010 and 2019, around half of court buildings were closed for budgetary reasons. Reopening old court buildings (where available) would have the advantage of them being inherently suitable for Crown Court trials; they would be able to 'hit the ground running' and conduct trials as they used to.

THE BEST SOLUTION

The 'jury question' is not a straightforward one. Having considered the options carefully, I would suggest that the best option is multi-faceted approach of opening closed buildings, setting up 'Nightingale' courts and continuing to hold virtual hearings. I set out my suggested approach below.

I would suggest that the 'Nightingale' courts option should be seriously pursued. We do not know at this time how many buildings are available, of course, but on its face, any suitable building will help to tackle the backlog.

Those court buildings that have been closed should be assessed, as to their suitability for opening, and opened where it is possible to do so.

Socially distanced trials can then be conducted in those court buildings and the 'Nightingale' courts – either by using more than one courtroom, or by setting up suitably large courtrooms so that all can remain one metre apart from each other.

In order to ensure that all possible space in court buildings is used for trials only, virtual hearings should remain in place for all pre-trial and post-trial hearings. Where, for whatever reason, either the Judge directs of his own motion – or parties to the case apply – for a particular hearing to be in person, then it may be so listed. However, the presumption should be that those hearings will be virtual unless directed otherwise. Provision should be made for the Judge in those cases to conduct the virtual hearing from his or her Chambers in the court, or another suitable place. This will free those courtrooms that are beset by long lists of short hearings.

I would certainly reject any idea that the use of a jury of twelve people should be temporarily suspended. This includes a rejection of any suggestion that the defendant be able to elect trial by Judge alone in certain circumstances. Whilst the right of the defendant to elect may have its advantages in normal situations, to introduce such a provision in the current climate carries the greatest risk that the defendant will not feel they have a free choice. After all, if they are facing a long delay should they hold out for a jury, but a faster resolution with a Judge alone, they may feel pressurised make a decision on the basis of that time factor.

In terms of removing the jury altogether, the right to a jury has been a fundamental one in England and Wales for centuries – for good reasons, as I touch upon above. World War Two did, it is true, demonstrate that the right may justifiably be infringed where circumstances necessitate it. I do not believe that we are in that position yet. We have the facilities to conduct socially distanced trials, in terms of court buildings. We have Judges available, whose sitting days were previously reduced for budgetary reasons. We have practitioners who are able and willing to return to work so long as the proper safety measures are in place. We have all the raw material available to continue our jury trial system without needing to curtail it.

It is true that opening closed courts and listing more Judicial sitting days may well require a significant financial injection. However, the proper running of a criminal justice system is essential to any fair society – quite simply, it is worth being put at the top of the priorities list. To ignore the options that are available, and instead opt to employ the cheaper option of doing away with the jury, would be a gravely worrying course of action for a country that prides itself on having a fair and just criminal system.

PART THREE

THE IMPACT OF COVID-19 ON JUDICIAL DECISIONS IN CRIMINAL CASES

CHAPTER SEVEN
COVID-19 AND DEPRIVATION OF LIBERTY CASES

This chapter considers the impact of the pandemic on prison conditions and, therefore, on sentencing decisions. It considers the recent caselaw and the guidance of the Sentencing Council.

OVERVIEW

We have considered both the impact of Covid-19 on criminal offences, and its impact on the working of the criminal courts. Finally, we shall consider the impact of Covid-19 on Judicial decisions in criminal cases. The key area that has been affected thus far is sentencing; despite the fact that it has been a matter of a few months since 'lockdown' was declared, we already have the benefit of Judicial and Sentencing Council Guidance.

The Judiciary has recognised that those in custody have been adversely affected by the arrival of the pandemic. Prison conditions are not as they were before the pandemic: the need for social distancing, restrictions on movement and general mitigation of risk have resulted in some prisoners being confined to their cells for periods of up to 23 hours a day.

For this reason, the guidance issued by the Courts and the Sentencing Council has encouraged Judges to take that into account when considering the impact of prison upon the defendant they are sentencing, and when considering whether it might be possible to suspend a sentence. It would be useful for any practitioner to have the guidance below at their fingertips, whilst the conditions in prisons remain the same.

The decision as to whether or not to grant bail may also be affected, and so I touch upon that below.

COVID-19 AND SENTENCING

The pandemic has had a direct impact on prison conditions. They have probably been best summarised in R v Manning (2020) EWCA Crim 592 at paragraph 41:

> "*We would mention one other factor of relevance. We are hearing this Reference at the end of April 2020, when the nation remains in lock-down as a result of the Covid-19 emergency. The impact of that emergency on prisons is well known. [...] Those in custody are, for example, confined to their cells for much longer periods than would otherwise be the case—currently, 23 hours a day. They are unable to receive visits. Both they and their families are likely to be anxious about the risk of the transmission of Covid-19.*"

Within that same paragraph 41, the Court stated:

> "*The current conditions in prisons represent a factor which can properly be taken into account in deciding whether to suspend a sentence. In accordance with established principles, any court will take into account the likely impact of a custodial sentence upon an offender and, where appropriate, upon others as well. Judges and magistrates can, therefore, and in our judgment should, keep in mind that the impact of a custodial sentence is likely to be heavier during the current emergency than it would otherwise be.*"

At paragraph 42:

> "*42. Applying ordinary principles, where a court is satisfied that a custodial sentence must be imposed, the likely impact of that sentence continues to be relevant to the further decisions as to its necessary length and whether it can be suspended ...*"

Taking into account the impact of a prison sentence upon the defendant is not in itself a new concept. Submissions might be advanced where the defendant suffers from a particular medical condition, or is of advanced age, for example. What is perhaps novel is placing before the Court mitigation that it is the general state of the prison conditions across the country that will make a custodial sentence harder on the defendant. *Manning* has, though, made it clear that this is a factor that should be taken into account.

It is important to note that it is not a factor to weigh in favour of suspending even those sentences that would certainly never otherwise be suspended. It is of relevance where the Judge might be considering whether or not to suspend a sentence. In that case, the heavier impact of current conditions in custody is a factor that might tip the balance in favour of a suspended sentence. Where suspending a sentence is not a realistic option, the Court will take the current conditions in prison into account when deciding the length of the custodial sentence.

This approach was confirmed in the case of *R v Jones* (2020) EWCA Crim 764. In that case, applying the case of *Manning*, the Court of Appeal reduced the appellant's sentence from 8 months' imprisonment to 6 months' imprisonment. In that case, the appellant had been sentenced just days before lockdown was imposed and prison conditions worsened. The Court of Appeal stated at paragraph 19:

> "*We are of the view that in the present, exceptional, circumstances it is appropriate to take the conditions under which the applicant is presently held in custody into account. We do not of course criticise the judge for the sentence imposed because the judge was wholly unaware of the change in prison conditions that would arise just days after the sentence was imposed.*"

The Court of Appeal Judges in *Jones* underlined, once more, the fact that the state of prison conditions during the pandemic may well be the determining factor in a case that would otherwise merit a longer sentence. In their last line of paragraph 19, the Judges make clear that the Crown Court Judge would have been entitled to pass the sentence that he did had the prison conditions not changed due to the pandemic. In the event, the pandemic was responsible for a two month reduction in the overall sentence.

The Sentencing Council has also recently published updated guidance on sentencing cases during the current pandemic[1]. This guidance references and affirms *Manning*:

> "*In deciding whether a custodial sentence is necessary, a court must follow the approach set out in the Sentencing Council's Imposition guideline. This guideline requires the court to consider first whether the custody threshold has been passed. It makes clear that even where the court decides that the custody threshold has been passed, it must go on to consider whether it is unavoidable that a custodial sentence be imposed. If a custodial sentence is unavoidable, the court must then decide what is the shortest term commen-*

1 Available at https://www.sentencingcouncil.org.uk/news/item/the-application-of-sentencing-principles-during-the-covid-19-emergency/, last accessed on 27 June 2020.

> *surate with the seriousness of the offence(s) and must consider whether the sentence can be suspended.*
>
> *In accordance with well-established principles, the court in answering those questions should take into account the likely impact of a custodial sentence upon the offender and, where appropriate, upon others such as children or other dependents.*
>
> *This has recently been confirmed by the decision in the case of Manning …*"

The Guidance also indicates that greater leniency may be given when determining the level of credit a defendant should get for his guilty plea:

> "*In addition, when applying the Reduction in Sentence for a Guilty Plea guideline, the court must consider the exceptions in that guideline. The exceptions include whether there were particular circumstances affecting the defendant's ability to understand the allegations or to receive the advice necessary before pleading guilty, or where the defendant pleads guilty to, and is then convicted of, a different offence from that originally charged. In making these considerations, the court must keep in mind the practical difficulties of defendants accessing legal advice during the present emergency.*"

It may well be, then, that a guilty plea entered after the preliminary hearings would still attract a substantial level of credit, should it be clear that the defendant could not have realistically accessed full legal advice any earlier.

COVID-19 AND BAIL

There is no explicit requirement, when reaching a bail decision, to take into account the impact of remand conditions on the applicant, as there is when sentencing them. The test is simply whether there is a 'real risk' of absconding, committing further offences, intimidating witnesses or of harm to the applicant themselves. However, that does not mean that Covid-19 has no conceivable effect on the decision to grant bail.

First, the backlog of trials means that any defendant on remand might be in custody far longer than before, awaiting their trial. As discussed in Chapter 4, the number of adjourned trials is only growing. Defendants might find themselves waiting a significant time for their trials to be heard. The problem then arises when the amount of time a defendant will spend on remand will likely exceed the likely sentence he will receive. He could, effectively, end up serving a longer sentence waiting for his trial than he would receive after a guilty verdict.

This is relevant when we consider Article 5 of the European Convention of Human Rights, and the right to a trial within a reasonable time when on remand:

> "***Article 5***
>
> *1. Everyone has the right to liberty and security of person. No one shall be deprived of his liberty save in the following cases and in accordance with a procedure prescribed by law:*
>
> *[...]*
>
> > *(c) the lawful arrest or detention of a person effected for the purpose of bringing him before the competent legal authority on*

> *reasonable suspicion of having committed an offence or when it is reasonably considered necessary to prevent his committing an offence or fleeing after having done so;*
>
> *[...]*
>
> *3. Everyone arrested or detained in accordance with the provisions of paragraph 1.c of this article shall be brought promptly before a judge or other officer authorised by law to exercise judicial power and shall be entitled to trial within a reasonable time or to release pending trial. Release may be conditioned by guarantees to appear for trial.*"

Paragraph 3 entitles the defendant on remand to be brought to trial within a reasonable time, or otherwise to release pending trial. In usual circumstances, the 'custody time limit' provision ensures that the defendant on remand is brought to trial within a reasonable time.

In the current circumstances, however, it may simply not be possible to list a trial within the usual custody time limits of a defendant remanded during lockdown. It is not inconceivable that a defendant remanded today might be waiting for over a year for his trial. That is the equivalent to two years spent in prison. Paragraph 3 does not give a specific period of time that would be considered 'unreasonable': to do so would be arbitrary and fail to reflect the nuances in each case. However, it could safely be argued that when the offence for which the defendant is awaiting trial is more than likely to attract a lesser sentence than the time the defendant will serve through his remand period waiting for that trial, the trial cannot have been brought within a reasonable time.

Secondly, the Judge has to consider whether there is a 'real risk' of absconding, committing further offences or interfering with witnesses. Arguably, that risk is reduced where there are national restrictions in place governing travel and contact with those outside your household.

Finally, all conditions must be necessary to achieve their aim, and proportionate interferences with the defendant's rights. This is another aspect that should be considered more carefully in light of the current pandemic. There might – for example - be a situation where the interference with a defendant's right to self-isolate is disproportionately intrusive when compared to the need to place electronic monitoring equipment on him. In that case, there may be an argument against the condition, even where there would ordinarily be no objection.

CONCLUSION

The sudden changes to both the criminal law and criminal procedure since 23 March 2020 have required quick, efficient reaction. Those of us working within the system at this time could be forgiven for focusing simply on the day to day issues that have arisen. Those are not insignificant. Matters such as ensuring that a particular online platform works, that a client is able to receive appropriate advice despite being unable to attend a hearing, and that offences brought under the Act and Regulations are correctly charged, are all essential to ensure as little disruption as possible in this new climate.

However now that the dust is settling somewhat, it is becoming clear that the effects of the current situation will reach far further than may have been thought in the early days of March 2020.

New offences have been built into the criminal law; that will mean that there may be people prosecuted for breaches of 'lockdown' rules even when the 'lockdown' period is truly over. There have been a number of pre-existing criminal offences that have seen a spike in occurrence during the current period. We may then see a larger number of prosecutions in those areas of crime.

The criminal courts have been dragged, suddenly and forcefully, into a virtual arena. Any short hearings that can be heard virtually is so listed; those that cannot are adjourned. At the time of writing, the virtual courts system has been running for three months. There is little report of widescale dissatisfaction. It may be, then, that virtual hearings can play a greater part in the future of the criminal courts than they did previously. The technology will need to have some improvements made to it, to address issues such as the lack of satisfactory ability to have client conferences and to implement a uniform virtual system, but on the whole, there seems to be no reason why virtual hearings cannot play a significant role in the criminal justice system.

Jury trials are, by far, the biggest problem at the current time. With a few exceptions, jury trials have been adjourned in their tens of thousands. The right to a trial within a reasonable time is a fundamental right of the criminal system and is duly enshrined in Article 6 of the European Convention on Human Rights. Aside from the very real worry as to the impact of long delays on the defendants, witnesses and complainants, there is the concern as to the impact on practitioners themselves. The criminal barrister's income is ideally made up of a healthy balance between short hearings - that are necessary but may often result in negligible profit or even loss once expenses are deducted – and longer trials, that pay the bulk of the case fee. Without trials reappearing soon, practitioners across the board could suffer. Many may not be able to sustain a practice, and will be forced to look into other practice areas or even other careers to earn an income.

We cannot allow the pandemic to strip defendants of their basic rights, force complainants and witnesses to wait an agonisingly long time to give evidence and plunge into financial ruin those who have made it their livelihoods to represent the prosecution and the defence. It is imperative that the 'jury question' be resolved as soon as realistically possible. Equally, in our haste to resolve it, we must not be callous with the treatment of fundamental rights, such as the right to trial by a jury of twelve of one's peers. To do so without proper consideration would be to put forward a clumsily constructed way of dealing with criminal trials, that could lead to many a defendant fearing they have been the victim of a miscarriage of justice.

All is not 'doom and gloom', though. With proper consideration, and genuine commitment from those responsible for funding the system, it may be that a better way of working emerges. First, if we can build effective virtual hearings into the system permanently, we reduce the need for barristers to travel halfway across the country for a loss-leading hearing, and we reduce the need for so much space to be taken up in a court building accommodating a list of short hearings. Quite conceivably, after all, the Judge could be in Chambers whilst all others attend remotely. Secondly, if more closed courts are re-opened to enable the resumption of jury trials, as well as the use of reconstituted buildings where needed, then we might be able to push through the backlog of jury trials. When the backlog is finally dealt with, it may be that the obvious benefits of keeping more court buildings open is recognised. More court buildings mean more trials can be heard at any one time, reducing waiting times and the need for warned lists, and that is a system which benefits all.

It is true that the exact impact of the current pandemic on the criminal justice system cannot be known with any certainty. There is certainly potential for the system to emerge from the crisis with improvements across the board. Time will tell whether that will happen; one can only hope that it does.

MORE BOOKS BY LAW BRIEF PUBLISHING

A selection of our other titles available now:-

'Covid-19, Homeworking and the Law – The Essential Guide to Employment and GDPR Issues' by Forbes Solicitors
'Covid-19, Force Majeure and Frustration of Contracts – The Essential Guide' by Keith Markham
'Covid-19 and Criminal Law – The Essential Guide' by Ramya Nagesh
'Covid-19 and Family Law in England and Wales – The Essential Guide' by Safda Mahmood
'Covid-19 and the Implications for Planning Law – The Essential Guide' by Bob Mc Geady & Meyric Lewis
'Covid-19, Residential Property, Equity Release and Enfranchisement – The Essential Guide' by Paul Sams and Louise Uphill
'Covid-19, Brexit and the Law of Commercial Leases – The Essential Guide' by Mark Shelton
'Covid-19 and the Law Relating to Food in the UK and Republic of Ireland – The Essential Guide' by Ian Thomas
'A Practical Guide to the General Data Protection Regulation (GDPR) – 2nd Edition' by Keith Markham
'Ellis on Credit Hire – Sixth Edition' by Aidan Ellis & Tim Kevan
'A Practical Guide to Working with Litigants in Person and McKenzie Friends in Family Cases' by Stuart Barlow
'Protecting Unregistered Brands: A Practical Guide to the Law of Passing Off' by Lorna Brazell
'A Practical Guide to Secondary Liability and Joint Enterprise Post-Jogee' by Joanne Cecil & James Mehigan
'A Practical Guide to the Pre-Action RTA Claims Protocol for Personal Injury Lawyers' by Antonia Ford
'A Practical Guide to Neighbour Disputes and the Law' by Alexander Walsh

'A Practical Guide to Forfeiture of Leases' by Mark Shelton
'A Practical Guide to Coercive Control for Legal Practitioners and Victims' by Rachel Horman
'A Practical Guide to Rights Over Airspace and Subsoil' by Daniel Gatty
'Tackling Disclosure in the Criminal Courts – A Practitioner's Guide' by Narita Bahra QC & Don Ramble
'A Practical Guide to the Law of Driverless Cars – Second Edition' by Alex Glassbrook, Emma Northey & Scarlett Milligan
'A Practical Guide to TOLATA Claims' by Greg Williams
'Artificial Intelligence – The Practical Legal Issues' by John Buyers
'A Practical Guide to the Law of Prescription in Scotland' by Andrew Foyle
'A Practical Guide to the Construction and Rectification of Wills and Trust Instruments' by Edward Hewitt
'A Practical Guide to the Law of Bullying and Harassment in the Workplace' by Philip Hyland
'How to Be a Freelance Solicitor: A Practical Guide to the SRA-Regulated Freelance Solicitor Model' by Paul Bennett
'A Practical Guide to Prison Injury Claims' by Malcolm Johnson
'A Practical Guide to the Small Claims Track' by Dominic Bright
'A Practical Guide to Advising Clients at the Police Station' by Colin Stephen McKeown-Beaumont
'A Practical Guide to Antisocial Behaviour Injunctions' by Iain Wightwick
'Practical Mediation: A Guide for Mediators, Advocates, Advisers, Lawyers, and Students in Civil, Commercial, Business, Property, Workplace, and Employment Cases' by Jonathan Dingle with John Sephton
'The Mini-Pupillage Workbook' by David Boyle
'A Practical Guide to Crofting Law' by Brian Inkster
'A Practical Guide to Spousal Maintenance' by Liz Cowell
'A Practical Guide to the Law of Domain Names and Cybersquatting' by Andrew Clemson
'A Practical Guide to the Law of Gender Pay Gap Reporting' by Harini Iyengar
'A Practical Guide to the Rights of Grandparents in Children Proceedings' by Stuart Barlow

'NHS Whistleblowing and the Law' by Joseph England
'Employment Law and the Gig Economy' by Nigel Mackay & Annie Powell
'A Practical Guide to Noise Induced Hearing Loss (NIHL) Claims' by Andrew Mckie, Ian Skeate, Gareth McAloon
'An Introduction to Beauty Negligence Claims – A Practical Guide for the Personal Injury Practitioner' by Greg Almond
'Intercompany Agreements for Transfer Pricing Compliance' by Paul Sutton
'Zen and the Art of Mediation' by Martin Plowman
'A Practical Guide to the SRA Principles, Individual and Law Firm Codes of Conduct 2019 – What Every Law Firm Needs to Know' by Paul Bennett
'A Practical Guide to Adoption for Family Lawyers' by Graham Pegg
'A Practical Guide to Industrial Disease Claims' by Andrew Mckie & Ian Skeate
'A Practical Guide to Redundancy' by Philip Hyland
'A Practical Guide to Vicarious Liability' by Mariel Irvine
'A Practical Guide to Applications for Landlord's Consent and Variation of Leases' by Mark Shelton
'A Practical Guide to Relief from Sanctions Post-Mitchell and Denton' by Peter Causton
'A Practical Guide to Equity Release for Advisors' by Paul Sams
'A Practical Guide to Unlawful Eviction and Harassment' by Stephanie Lovegrove
'A Practical Guide to the Law Relating to Food' by Ian Thomas
'A Practical Guide to Financial Services Claims' by Chris Hegarty
'The Law of Houses in Multiple Occupation: A Practical Guide to HMO Proceedings' by Julian Hunt
'A Practical Guide to Unlawful Eviction and Harassment' by Stephanie Lovegrove
'A Practical Guide to Solicitor and Client Costs' by Robin Dunne
'Occupiers, Highways and Defective Premises Claims: A Practical Guide Post-Jackson – 2nd Edition' by Andrew Mckie
'A Practical Guide to Financial Ombudsman Service Claims' by Adam Temple & Robert Scrivenor
'A Practical Guide to Advising Schools on Employment Law' by Jonathan Holden

'A Practical Guide to Running Housing Disrepair and Cavity Wall Claims: 2nd Edition' by Andrew Mckie & Ian Skeate
'A Practical Guide to Holiday Sickness Claims – 2nd Edition' by Andrew Mckie & Ian Skeate
'Arguments and Tactics for Personal Injury and Clinical Negligence Claims' by Dorian Williams
'A Practical Guide to QOCS and Fundamental Dishonesty' by James Bentley
'A Practical Guide to Drone Law' by Rufus Ballaster, Andrew Firman, Eleanor Clot
'A Practical Guide to Compliance for Personal Injury Firms Working With Claims Management Companies' by Paul Bennett
'A Practical Guide to the Landlord and Tenant Act 1954: Commercial Tenancies' by Richard Hayes & David Sawtell
'A Practical Guide to Dog Law for Owners and Others' by Andrea Pitt
'RTA Allegations of Fraud in a Post-Jackson Era: The Handbook – 2nd Edition' by Andrew Mckie
'RTA Personal Injury Claims: A Practical Guide Post-Jackson' by Andrew Mckie
'On Experts: CPR35 for Lawyers and Experts' by David Boyle
'An Introduction to Personal Injury Law' by David Boyle
'A Practical Guide to Chronic Pain Claims' by Pankaj Madan
'A Practical Guide to Claims Arising from Fatal Accidents' by James Patience
'A Practical Guide to Subtle Brain Injury Claims' by Pankaj Madan

These books and more are available to order online direct from the publisher at www.lawbriefpublishing.com, where you can also read free sample chapters. For any queries, contact us on 0844 587 2383 or mail@lawbriefpublishing.com.

Our books are also usually in stock at www.amazon.co.uk with free next day delivery for Prime members, and at good legal bookshops such as Wildy & Sons.

We are regularly launching new books in our series of practical day-to-day practitioners' guides. Visit our website and join our free newsletter to be kept informed and to receive special offers, free chapters, etc.

You can also follow us on Twitter at www.twitter.com/lawbriefpub.

www.ingramcontent.com/pod-product-compliance
Lightning Source LLC
LaVergne TN
LVHW022108200926
848481LV00003B/1099
9781913715212